How to Lead It: Primary Science

Other titles from Bloomsbury Education

How to Lead It: Primary English by Tricia Moss and Sallie Stanton
How to Lead It: Primary Maths by Shannen Doherty
How to Lead It: Primary History by Alex Pethick
How to Lead It: Primary Geography by Emma Lennard
The Curriculum Compendium by Rae Snape
What Every Teacher Needs to Know by Jade Pearce

How to Lead It: Primary Science

Kirsty Simkin
Series editor: Jon Hutchinson

BLOOMSBURY EDUCATION
LONDON OXFORD NEW YORK NEW DELHI SYDNEY

BLOOMSBURY EDUCATION
Bloomsbury Publishing Plc
50 Bedford Square, London WC1B 3DP, UK
Bloomsbury Publishing Ireland Limited
29 Earlsfort Terrace, Dublin 2, D02 AY28, Ireland

BLOOMSBURY, BLOOMSBURY EDUCATION and the Diana logo are trademarks of
Bloomsbury Publishing Plc

First published in Great Britain, 2025 by Bloomsbury Publishing Plc
This edition published in Great Britain, 2025 by Bloomsbury Publishing Plc

Text copyright © Kirsty Simkin, 2025
Kirsty Simkin has asserted her rights under the Copyright, Designs and Patents Act,
1988, to be identified as Author of this work

Bloomsbury Publishing Plc does not have any control over, or responsibility for, any
third-party websites referred to or in this book. All internet addresses given in this
book were correct at the time of going to press. The author and publisher regret any
inconvenience caused if addresses have changed or sites have ceased to exist, but can
accept no responsibility for any such changes

Photos on page 120 left © Nagel Photography / Shutterstock.com; centre
© Lucie Bartikova / Shutterstock.com; right © pervaiziq / Shutterstock.com
Quotes from Ofsted documents and the Department for Education used in this
publication are approved under an Open Government Licence: https://www.nationalarchi
ves.gov.uk/doc/open-government-licence/version/3/

All rights reserved. No part of this publication may be: i) reproduced or transmitted in
any form, electronic or mechanical, including photocopying, recording or by means of
any information storage or retrieval system without prior permission in writing from
the publishers; or ii) used or reproduced in any way for the training, development or
operation of artificial intelligence (AI) technologies, including generative AI technologies.
The rights holders expressly reserve this publication from the text and data mining
exception as per Article 4(3) of the Digital Single Market Directive
(EU) 2019/790

A catalogue record for this book is available from the British Library

ISBN: PB: 978-1-8019-9626-6; ePDF: 978-1-8019-9627-3; ePub: 978-1-8019-9629-7
2 4 6 8 10 9 7 5 3 1 (paperback)
Cover design by Sophie Gordon

Typeset by Newgen Knowledge Works Pvt. Ltd., Chennai, India
Printed and bound in the UK by CPI Group (UK) Ltd., Croydon, CR0 4YY

To find out more about our authors and books visit www.bloomsbury.com
and sign up for our newsletters

For product safety related questions contact productsafety@bloomsbury.com

Contents

1. Leading science 1

2. Getting the best from research evidence 11

3. Big ideas in science 23

4. Curriculum design principles 39

5. How to plan a curriculum 51

6. Assessment: what do my pupils know? 63

7. Explanations and modelling 79

8. Vocabulary 89

9. Practical science 101

10. Dialogue 115

11. Disciplinary literacy 129

12. Engagement in science 141

13. Implementing change 159

Bibliography 175
Index 183

1 Leading science

Being a subject leader is one of the best jobs you can have in a school. Being in charge of the strategic direction of a subject, promoting its value across the school, guiding curriculum and supporting staff to be excellent teachers in your subject are all worthy and rewarding parts of the role.

Taking on responsibility for leading science may be your first step into leadership – and, like many primary teachers, you may not have a strong science background. However, this need not be a barrier to leading excellent primary science. This book has been written to support you to develop expertise in both science teaching and leadership.

I started my teacher training at a brilliant school. I was blown away by the dedicated staff, the enormous care they had for all the pupils and the high quality of teaching and learning. Even fantastic schools have areas for development though. It quickly came to my attention that an excellent science curriculum was a missing piece of the puzzle.

No other staff member had a science-based degree, and science was taught as a 'science week' once a term. That was the landscape in which I eagerly took up the role of science lead. Now, eight years later, things are in a very different place. I have learned many lessons while leading and transforming science education in my own school, and also while working with other schools to revamp their science offer too. This book is intended to be the guide I wish I'd had when I first started my subject leadership journey. I hope it will help many current, or aspiring, science subject leaders.

In this chapter, we are going to introduce science as a subject, covering current aims, challenges and inequities in the science-education landscape. We will also take a look at the key aspects of the role of a primary science leader working within this landscape.

Aims of primary science education

Let's start at the very beginning. What is science, and what are the aims of a high-quality primary science education?

Science is both a body of knowledge (things we have already discovered) and a process of acquiring new knowledge (through observation and experimentation) about the natural world. Science education is a crucial part of the National Curriculum for England. Since the Education Reform Act of 1988, it has been considered a core subject alongside mathematics and English. However, science is much more than just a compulsory subject: it sparks wonder in young minds, encouraging curiosity and exploration of the world. It helps pupils to develop a range of skills that broad applications.

The primary science curriculum covers three main areas:

- scientific knowledge and ideas across biology, chemistry, and physics
- the methods and skills of science used to answer scientific questions
- how science applies to and impacts the wider world, both now and in the future.

The key aims of science education have been debated, and different curriculums may emphasise different aims. Below is a list of some of the most important purposes of science education.

A good science education should help pupils:

- understand the world around them
- comprehend how science applies to their own lives and society
- learn how scientific knowledge is established through investigation
- appreciate important scientific contributions from the past, such as the theory of evolution
- recognise science's role in addressing global challenges such as climate change.

The role of a primary science leader

Your role as a primary science leader is to ensure that the pupils in your school have a science education that meets the aims laid out above. To do this, you will use an effective curriculum inside and outside the classroom, and plan improvements that both raise standards for pupils and support colleagues to teach science better.

Five key concepts for subject leads

Let's break down what this means by looking at the role in five key areas.

1. Curriculum development

Developing your school's science curriculum will involve:

- refining and regularly reviewing the subject's vision, aims and purpose
- overseeing teachers' own curriculum planning to ensure well-sequenced content for pupil progress
- ensuring consistent curriculum implementation, including adequate timetable allocation
- implementing effective assessment systems to monitor pupil progress and curriculum impact
- ensuring an inclusive curriculum that supports all pupils, including those with special educational needs and disabilities (SEND) and English as an additional language (EAL)
- taking overall responsibility for pupil achievement and standards in science
- keeping up to date on relevant research related to science teaching.

2. Resourcing

Planning and acquiring resources for your subject will involve:

- managing the subject budget effectively, spending it in ways that add value and enhance learning
- ensuring the availability of necessary equipment for practical science teaching
- pursuing additional funding from external sources, when needed
- supporting literacy departments with science-related books and materials
- providing access to safety guidance and risk-assessment information
- auditing and updating resources to align with curriculum and pupil needs.

3. Monitoring teaching and learning

Assessing how well your subject is being implemented, and how well it is delivered across the school, can be done by:

- utilising data analysis
- taking learning walks
- moderating assessment
- observing lessons
- checking planning
- engaging with pupil voice, using informal interviews with small groups of children, conversations with the school council or pupils' questionnaires
- reviewing a small sample of pupils' books from each class.

4. Supporting colleagues

You can foster a supportive working environment by:

- leading a cohesive team, regularly updating teachers on subject developments
- guiding staff through teaching, learning, resources and planning
- offering feedback and professional development opportunities, based on classroom observations
- assisting with accurate assessments and moderation processes.

5. Raising the profile of science and enrichment

Promoting engagement with your subject for pupils, colleagues and parents and carers alike could include:

- running science clubs
- organising science trips
- promoting science competitions and pupil leadership
- hosting science events and school visits, for example science fairs, science weeks, or visits from scientists or local industry leaders

- considering how to involve parents and carers and keep them informed, for example through a school website, newsletters, interactive homework tasks and projects, or 'family learning' nights.

Finding focus and prioritising

When laid out in full, the role can seem vast – but don't be daunted! Realistically, a science lead cannot implement everything at once (and there will be more on this in Chapter 13).

The key is to prioritise. Each academic year, a subject lead should decide their strategic focuses for the year ahead. For example, one year the focus might be on creating a coherent curriculum and supporting teachers to implement it. The next year, you might focus on improving teachers' subject knowledge through PD, and ensuring each year group goes on a science-related trip. The year after that, you might focus on ensuring all classes have access to a wide range of science texts, and develop a science club and student committee.

The lists under the five key concepts above can help you to audit what is working well in your school and where there may be areas for development. They can also be used as a self-audit tool, helping you to reflect on which areas feel more comfortable and which might need some support or development.

The current educational landscape

In the Early Years Foundation Stage (EYFS), pupils embark on their formal science-education journey. This stage is rooted in the 'Understanding the world: The natural world' area of learning, laying the groundwork by introducing foundational knowledge. Through a number of rich contexts, pupils learn a diverse vocabulary. Through experimentation and play, they are encouraged to problem-solve, observe, predict, think, make decisions and talk about the world around them. This lays the groundwork for scientific concepts and skills that will be further explored in subsequent years.

At primary school, the content that pupils learn is outlined by national curriculums. These organise learning into topics, such as plants, everyday materials and light. The National Curriculum for England also lays out statutory requirements for 'working scientifically', and the Scottish Curriculum of Excellence for 'inquiry and investigative skills'. These recommendations direct how pupils may work this way as part of each topic.

Current educational challenges

Despite science being a core subject, there are worries that it isn't getting enough attention in primary schools. The removal of primary-level NC tests in 2009 is thought by some to have led to reduced curriculum time for science and a devaluing of science by senior leaders. Others may blame strain on school budgets and difficulties of balancing the demands of other subjects.

A lack of focus on science

The attainment data below highlight that there is a lack of focus on science across many UK schools.

National attainment data

- In 2018, only 21.2% of Year 6 pupils reached the expected standard in science in the national sample tests.
- This is nearly 7% lower than in 2014.
- Just over half of the pupils in Years 7 and 8 feel ready for secondary school science (Bianchi et al., 2021).
- Pupils often spend time engaging in 'fun activities' at the cost of deep understanding of scientific concepts (Bianchi et al., 2021).

International comparisons

- England ranked 15th out of 80 countries in science PISA tests in 2022.
- Overall, the science score has dropped from 2012 to 2022.

Challenges at school

As a subject lead, it is important to be realistic about the challenges facing primary science education today. It is part of our role to improve attainment data, and many of us will need to do so in the context of the challenges below. Timetable challenges:

- 13-16% of primary schools don't teach science weekly (Wellcome Trust, 2017).

- Ofsted reports that, in most schools, English and maths are getting disproportionate amounts of curriculum time, especially for SATs preparation (Ofsted, 2021).
- Many schools teach science alongside humanities subjects under the banner of 'topic' work.

School leadership challenges:

- Only 41% of schools feel they have enough budget for science resources.
- Only 30% of senior leaders think science is 'very important', compared to 84% for maths and 83% for English.

In light of these data, it is likely that the most important task for many subject leads will be to advocate for science as an important subject, in order to ensure that adequate budget and teaching time can be allocated. It can be helpful here to remember (and to remind senior leadership) that science is considered a core subject, alongside English and maths, in the National Curriculum.

Mapping out your curriculum (see Chapters 4 and 5) and presenting this to senior leadership can be a good starting point. It can help you to plan together how much timetable time and budget will be needed to cover the curriculum adequately.

Inequities in science education

Across all subjects, we as educators face the challenge of closing attainment gaps between pupils from different backgrounds. It is important to be aware of the data on how these gaps manifest in science.

Data show that there are inequalities in science education based on gender, race and socio-economic disadvantage.

Socio-economic disadvantage

- In the last six years, pupils eligible for free school meals have been shown to perform at significantly lower levels than their peers (DfE, 2020).
- Disadvantaged pupils make less progress in science at every stage of education (Nunes et al., 2017).

- These pupils are less likely to take science subjects at A-level and beyond (Nunes et al., 2017).

Gender disparities

- At A level and degree level, STEM subjects (science, technology, engineering and mathematics) show gender imbalances. Women are overrepresented in biological science and underrepresented in physics, engineering and computing (Archer et al., 2023).
- In 2020–2021, women made up only 32% of STEM-degree undergraduates, in comparison to 62% of non-STEM degree undergraduates (Archer et al., 2023).

Racial disparities

- Black students are underrepresented in STEM subjects at degree level. The lowest representation is in physics (2.6%) and highest is in computing (11.0%) (Archer et al., 2023).

These statistics are incredibly important for a primary subject lead to be aware of. We have the absolute privilege of guiding pupils through the part of the educational journey in which they are just beginning to form their views about science and themselves. We have the opportunity to show all pupils that science is enjoyable, that it is relevant to their lives, that they can be successful and that they are represented. If we want to change these statistics at A level, degree level and in STEM-based careers, we need to tackle pupils' perceptions of science as soon as we start to teach it.

How this book can support you

Throughout this book, we will explore different aspects of the primary science curriculum in more detail, giving you a strong foundation from which to teach and lead the subject. You will find:

- examples of best practice from across key stages
- fictional case studies for further exemplification
- suggestions for staff professional development

- reflection questions to help you structure your thoughts and identify next steps
- follow-up reading and resources if you want to explore a particular area further.

In the next chapter, we draw insights from cognitive science together with evidence related to the practice of science teaching. We then look at how you can take an evidence-based approach yourself.

We next look at curriculum design in science. This involves looking at the 'big ideas' in science (Chapter 3), the key principles of curriculum design (Chapter 4) and a step-by-step guide for planning your science curriculum (Chapter 5).

You will then find detailed chapters on specific areas of the subject: assessment (Chapter 6), modelling and explanations (Chapter 7), vocabulary (Chapter 8), practical science (Chapter 9), dialogue (Chapter 10) and disciplinary literacy (Chapter 11).

In Chapter 12, we explore strategies to address some of the challenges laid out in this introduction. We look at how to increase all pupils' engagement with science through citizen research and broad representation within the curriculum.

We finish with guidance on implementing improvement and change (Chapter 13).

Chapter summary

- Science leadership is a rewarding role that offers the chance to shape the future of science education. As a science lead, you have the power to inspire curiosity, foster innovation and ignite a lifelong love of learning in your pupils.
- You have the ability to make science accessible and enjoyable for all pupils. By addressing inequities and tailoring your approach to your context, you can ensure that every pupil, regardless of background, sees themselves represented in science and believes in their potential to succeed.
- You have the chance to develop an inclusive and rigorous curriculum that prepares all your pupils for future science learning, and allows them to live informed and healthy lives.
- Through strategic planning and prioritisation, you can gradually implement positive changes in your school. Whether it's improving resources,

enhancing teaching methods or introducing exciting science events, your efforts can lead to significant improvements over time.
- By advocating for science and raising its profile in your school, you can inspire the next generation of scientists, engineers and innovators.

Questions for reflection

- How much science is there in the timetable at our school? Is this purely science, or cross-curricular work?
- What are our pupils' attitudes to science? Do they enjoy it? Do they feel capable? Can they see themselves as scientists? Does this vary by demographic?
- Does science teaching currently reflect our whole-school vision for science?
- How does attainment in science compare with other core subjects for all pupils?

Explore further

- The Royal Society's Vision for science and mathematics education (2014): https://royalsociety.org/-/media/education/policy/vision/reports/vision-full-report-20140625.pdf
- The Wellcome Trust's 'State of the nation' report of primary science education (2020): https://wellcome.org/reports/state-nation-report-uk-primary-science-education
- Ofsted's Research review series: science (2021): https://www.gov.uk/government/publications/research-review-series-science/research-review-series-science

2 Getting the best from research evidence

> As a science subject lead, your core responsibility is to ensure high-quality teaching and good pupil outcomes in your subject. It is important that you base your decisions and practice upon evidence, using robust and reliable educational research to decide which are the most effective strategies for your setting.
>
> If you are new to subject leadership, that can seem a daunting task. However, the principles and resources laid out in this chapter aim to increase your confidence in reviewing research. They also provide you with a list of great go-to sources of evidence-based practice.

Guiding principles

To implement a new strategy or change effectively as a subject leader, you will need to make evidence-informed decisions. These could draw on both external evidence, such as research, and internal data from your own context about what has and has not worked in the past. The decisions come with an opportunity cost: the more time that is devoted to less-effective strategies, the less time there is to spend on more-effective ones. Therefore, we need to invest time to select the right solutions. The following approaches can be helpful in guiding decisions.

- **Prioritise large-scale studies**: Focus on research with substantial sample sizes. How an intervention worked for the pupils within a study is irrelevant if the same intervention is unlikely to work for your own pupils. Bigger samples tend to allow for more generalisable conclusions, leading to interventions appropriate for a wider range of learners.
- **Consider the consistency of the participants**: A large sample size doesn't automatically guarantee high-quality research. You should also examine the participant selection process and drop-out rates: long-term studies based on primary pupils are prone to changes in participants as

pupils and/or teachers move schools. Much research is also conducted on secondary-school pupils and undergraduates, so be cautious of applying findings about older pupils to those in primary or EYFS.

- **Compare contexts**: It is always important to look at context when putting good ideas into practice. Even when research shows something works well, what worked before doesn't guarantee future success (Major & Higgins, 2019). You should also think carefully about whether particular ideas are right for your situation. Your school might have special challenges that could make a new idea harder to use, for example, and you might need to do some preparation work to help it succeed. Before introducing a new idea, consider if it's possible for you, if you can afford it, and if you can keep it going. Often, it's easier to change what you're already doing instead of starting something completely new. This can save money and make it easier for people to accept and use a new idea. We will explore how to implement ideas from research successfully in Chapter 13.

- **Be wary of simplification**: Research that has been distilled into bite-sized chunks can lead us to decisions we believe are perfect fits for our schools. However, we should remember that broadly generalised results, especially those summarised without nuance, can only really give us an 'average effect' impression.

- **Don't trust results implicitly**: We should be mindful that all findings are built on a body of research that can be later questioned as more research studies are published. The dynamic nature of research means that leaders may need to keep updating their understanding. The best way to keep on top of relevant updates is to sign up the newsletters of trusted organisations (some of which are recommended below). This way you will get a regular reminder to engage with the newest findings.

- **Steer clear of educational fallacies**: The field of education is rife with myths, misconceptions and outdated ideas – for example, that pupils will learn better if they discover things for themselves, or that repetition is the surest way to secure understanding. Many of these persist despite being disproven (De Bruyckere et al., 2015). While you can't be aware of all of the fallacies, familiarising yourself with some common ones can save time, helping you to focus on more-promising approaches. (See the 'Explore further' section at the end of this chapter for some recommended reading on this.)

If you are a subject leader who is new to appraising evidence, you might want to start by looking at the Institute for Effective Education's 'Engaging with evidence guide', which breaks down different types of evidence and their limitations (Haslam & Shaw, 2019). The website 'That's a Claim!' (www.thatsaclaim.org/educational) is also helpful for bitesize explainers on different aspects of educational research.

Primary education sources and guidance

There are several notable challenges that make accessing, analysing and interpreting evidence difficult for those of us who work in schools. Lack of time to read and digest research, and difficulty interpreting the scientific jargon in research papers, are challenges familiar to many of us.

A good starting point is to look at what organisations who commission and conduct research have found to be effective. These organisations often digest research for educators into more-accessible formats and collate research into summaries. While keeping the guiding principles in mind, you may find the following evidence bases useful.

The Education Endowment Foundation (EEF)

The EEF is an independent charity that was set up to improve educational attainment levels of pupils from lower socio-economic backgrounds in England. The Foundation helps schools, colleges and early-years settings improve outcomes through the better use of evidence. This may be through their guidance reports, which review the evidence base for a range of strategies developed to support specific areas. Alternatively, it may be through research into the efficacy of specific strategies.

- Their guidance reports *Improving Primary Science* (2024) and *Improving Secondary Science* (2018) are productive starting points for science leads.
- The *Teaching and Learning Toolkit* (2021) is also helpful when thinking about curriculum and lesson design, as well as how to support teachers to become more effective in their practice.
- *A School's Guide to Implementation* (2024) provides clear structures and systems that can help us when implementing new strategies in our schools.

The Chartered College of Teaching

The Chartered College of Teaching is a professional body for teachers. Membership gives access to research, resources and the journal *Impact*. The College produces evidence summaries that review and collate research into short digests, and the journal has regular contributions from practitioners as well as researchers.

The Institute for Education Sciences (IES)

The IES is the independent, non-partisan statistics, research and evaluation arm of the US Department of Education. They conduct reviews on individual studies and grant access to a range of useful practice guides and intervention reports.

Science-specific resources

As science teachers and subject leads, we are lucky to have some really great resources available to us from subject associations and other educational organisations.

ORGANISATION AND SUMMARY OF RESOURCES	TIPS FOR USING THESE RESOURCES AS A SUBJECT LEADER
Association for Science Education (ASE) • PD sessions and events • Guidance documents for a range of topics • Primary science journal	I advise signing up to the science journal, which will help you to stay up to date with relevant research. The ASE also offers a wide range of PD and other events, at which you can improve your own science knowledge and subject leadership skills, and share practice with other science subject leaders.
Royal Society of Biology (RSB) • Awards and competitions for pupils • Ideas for biology-related practical activities	Including an element of practical science is important across all the subject domains, but teachers sometimes get caught up in comparative-testing experiments and neglect the wealth of other practical activities. Often, biology is the area of science in which the least practical work occurs. The RSB is a great starting point if you're looking for ideas for practical biology activities.

ORGANISATION AND SUMMARY OF RESOURCES	TIPS FOR USING THESE RESOURCES AS A SUBJECT LEADER
Royal Society of Chemistry (RSC) • STEM-career-related resources • Resources to support chemistry practical work • Video demonstrations	The RSC should be a starting point if you are planning how to increase subject knowledge in chemistry. I suggest having a look through their website and primary resources, and sharing these with classroom teachers.
Institute of Physics (IOP) • Teaching resources • Bank of misconceptions and ways to challenge them	The IOP is a good resource for increasing subject knowledge in physics. It is mostly geared towards secondary science, but some resources are also relevant to primary science teaching. As with the RSC, I suggest having a look through their website and resources, and sharing these with classroom teachers.
STEM Learning • PD for subject leads • STEM Ambassadors programme • Large bank of teaching resources	I advise that you familiarise yourself with the teaching resources, aiming to share anything you think is useful with your colleagues. The fantastic STEM Ambassadors programme allows you to organise for a scientist to come and visit your school to host a range of session types. The quality of their residential PD course is also very high: I definitely suggest signing up to one as a new or developing subject lead.
Primary Science Teaching Trust (PSTT) • Free quarterly magazine on primary science teaching • TAPS guidance and resources • Guidance documents and resources	These resources are helpful for any subject leader who wishes to further their understanding of science assessment practices, or who is looking to implement new science assessment policies in their school.
Ogden Trust • Impressive primary physics resources	This is one of my favourite places to go for primary physics resources. I recommend that you familiarise yourself with what they offer and share their resources with classroom teachers. They have a particularly good set of 'how to' resources for science leaders: for example, how to create primary science displays or how to run a science fair.

ORGANISATION AND SUMMARY OF RESOURCES	TIPS FOR USING THESE RESOURCES AS A SUBJECT LEADER
PLAN: Planning for Assessment • Curriculum progression documents • Examples of work • PD for subject leads to use with teachers	Having a clear codification and progression of key scientific vocabulary is challenging at a whole-school level, but the PLAN resources provide an excellent starting point by mapping out that language. This vocabulary can be added to medium-term plans, and you can work with teachers to ensure it is thoughtfully introduced in lessons and used by pupils in both their discussions and written work. Sharing this document during professional development sessions can prompt rich discussion about how the terms are defined and how their use develops. It will also enable you to ensure that terms aren't being used in inconsistent or incoherent ways.
Royal Institute • Potential for science visits and performances for schools (and ways to apply for grants for these) • Bank of videos and resources for practical science activities	Part of being a science leader is inspiring awe, wonder and love for the subject. I have yet to see more awe and wonder in the faces of my pupils than after a science show from the Royal Institute. Their bank of practical activities is also very well suited to home learning and extra-curricular projects as well as class work.
Explorify • Expertise from The Wellcome Trust, the PSTT and STEM Learning • Bank of activities that inspire questioning, deepen thinking and extend reasoning skills	I suggest that every science teacher signs up (for free) to Explorify, which provides a range of high-quality classroom resources and stimuli linked to national curriculums. They prompt high-quality talk and opportunities for pupils to reason in science. You could draw on the resources for ideas during your curriculum planning, or introduce them to teachers to support their implementation of the curriculum.

Case study: engaging with primary education sources and guidance

Fey has taken over as science lead in a two-form-entry primary school in Swindon. Her line manager has asked her to come up with an action plan for how to improve science across the school. Fey is relatively new to subject leadership and feels quite overwhelmed by this task.

She decides to start by exploring what the EEF have to say about improving primary science.

Having read the EEF's recommendations, Fey then sends a questionnaire out to teachers. It asks them to self-audit and identify which of the EEF's recommendations they feel they need the most support with. Assessment comes up as an area in which teachers do not feel confident.

Fey finds that the EEF guidance signposts an assessment approach called the Teacher Assessment in Primary Science (TAPS), and she explores this further. She finds that it is a rigorously evaluated approach that has demonstrated a positive impact of two months' additional progress in pupils' learning. It is specifically geared towards primary pupils.

Fey looks through the different strategies for collecting evidence of pupil learning that are exemplified on TAPs. She finds several examples of schools using videos of pupils explaining scientific concepts, which teachers use as a record and for assessment of the pupils' science knowledge. She thinks these would fit her context well, as many pupils find writing difficult, and this could be a barrier to them performing well in written assessments.

Fey summarises the TAPS approach, and prepares some examples of the video-record concept. She has a meeting with her line manager to discuss the best way to implement this new approach. She schedules a PD session with colleagues to introduce the benefits of both approaches.

What does the research say about cognitive science?

It's crucial for all subject leads and teachers to have a solid grasp of cognitive science and to stay current with its research findings on learning processes. These insights should be the foundation for all our teaching and learning strategies.

In his book *Why Don't Students Like School?* (2021), D. T. Willingham draws on the simple model of memory propounded by A. D. Baddeley and G. Hitch (1974). He explains the theoretical model and its impact for teaching in the classroom.

Here's a concise overview:

- **Working memory** acts as our brain's processing centre, briefly holding small amounts of new information. On average, an adult can hold and actively process about four chunks of new information in their working memory at a time. For children, it's likely to be fewer.
- **Learning** occurs when we successfully move new information from working memory into long-term memory.
- **Cognitive overload** can hinder or halt learning if working memory becomes overwhelmed. This happens when we're faced with too much new information to process simultaneously.
- **Optimising load** means reducing cognitive load that's unrelated to new key learning (such as new rules for a game) in order to increase capacity for essential cognitive load. This could be assisted by linking new content with information already stored in long-term memory, as this doesn't take up lots of working memory power.
- **Long-term memory** organises and stores information in structures called 'schemas'. These schemas can range from simple, containing just a few pieces of information, to highly complex, encompassing a vast quantity of data. The capacity of long-term memory may be finite.

Once information is stored in the long-term memory, it is accessed by the process of retrieval. All teachers should also be familiar with research on retrieval practice, as explained, for example, by Pashler et al. (2007):

- **Frequent recall** of learned material can enhance pupils' retention. The act of retrieving information reinforces the information in memory and reduces the likelihood of forgetting.
- **Spaced retrieval** is the most effective form of retrieval. Retrieval is most effective when pupils have started to forget the material: this requires more mental effort during recall, thereby strengthening memory connections. For optimal results, retrieval practice should be spread out over time rather than concentrated in a single session.

This research helps us to understand how learning occurs and has several implications for the classroom:

- **Implementing targeted planning**: Pupils need to concentrate on essential knowledge, skills and concepts. Teachers should be directed and assisted to design activities that direct pupils' focus to these core elements.
- **Building on existing knowledge**: Pupils understand new ideas by relating them to what they already know. Planning should be shaped by assessing and building upon pupils' prior knowledge.
- **Managing cognitive demands**: Pupils' working memory can easily become overwhelmed with new information. Teachers should be guided in how to be mindful of the cognitive load they impose, and plan should introduce new material in manageable segments.
- **Fostering fluency**: To develop deep understanding and fluency, pupils need to revisit and apply important content regularly. Plans should include frequent reviews, retrieval practice and ample opportunities for pupils to apply what they've learned.
- **Adjusting support levels**: As pupils develop a more-sophisticated understanding in a subject area, they require less guidance. Teachers should be encouraged to assess pupil understanding continuously, and be allowed the flexibility to adjust their levels of support accordingly, matching it to pupils' growing expertise.

> ### Case study: drawing on cognitive science for long-term planning
>
> Martin is a science leader in a four-form-entry school in Berkshire. He has taken on the role this year and his first aim is to ensure high-quality retrieval practice in all science classrooms.
>
> One of the most important aspects of this is deciding which areas to prioritise, in terms of pupils' long-term recall. For example, during lessons on the physics of light in Lower Key Stage 2 (LKS2), the priority is for pupils to remember that light travels in straight lines and that it reflects off some surfaces.
>
> Martin spends time adjusting the long- and medium-term plans so that it is explicit for teachers what the most important knowledge is in each unit. He then supports teachers to build weekly quizzes into their lessons. These include key questions on the core knowledge that began as multiple choice and then required more open-ended responses.
>
> He encourages teachers to include these same questions in recap quizzes in later years. This ensures that retrieval of core concepts is occurring across year groups, not just within a year group.

Chapter summary

- Base decisions on robust and reliable educational research, considering both external evidence and internal data from your own context.
- When evaluating research, focus on large-scale studies with consistency of participants, be sure to consider studies' contexts, be wary of simplification and the fallibility of researchers, and be aware of common educational myths and misconceptions.
- Utilise resources and guides from reputable organisations like the EEF and the Chartered College of Teaching to help assess and interpret research findings.

- Evaluate the fit of potential strategies to your specific school context, considering feasibility, cost-effectiveness and sustainability before implementation.
- Having a secure grasp of key cognitive science is important for subject leads, and should guide decisions.

Questions for reflection

- In what ways are we currently considering the specific context of our school when implementing new teaching strategies?
- Which of the science-specific resources mentioned in the chapter are we currently using, and which new ones could we explore to enhance your teaching and subject leadership?
- How well do we understand principles of cognitive science, such as working-memory limitations and retrieval practice, and apply them in our science lessons?

Example PD session: optimising cognitive load

Here is an example of what a PD session on optimising cognitive load could look like.

TIMING SUGGESTION	SESSION GUIDANCE
10 mins	Introduce the model of working memory, and explain the concept of optimising load: reducing cognitive load that's unrelated to new key learning in order to increase capacity for essential cognitive load.
15 mins	Give teachers some example tasks and ask them to identify which ones involve high levels of unnecessary cognitive load.
10 mins	Ask teachers, in pairs, to reflect on the tasks they have planned for the week ahead with cognitive load in mind. Prompt teachers to make any edits, and feed back to the group.

Explore further

- *The researchED Guide to Education Myths: An evidence-informed guide for teachers* (2019), edited by Craig Barton and Tom Bennett
- Oliver Caviglioli's blog *What is cognitive load theory?*: https://www.teachwire.net/news/what-is-cognitive-load-theory/
- The Centre for Education Statistics and Evaluation's *Cognitive load theory in practice: Examples for the classroom* (2018): https://khsbpp.wordpress.com/wp-content/uploads/2018/11/cognitive_load_theory_practice_guide_aa.pdf
- *What every teacher needs to know about psychology* (2016) by David Didau and Nick Rose
- *How learning happens: seminal works in educational psychology and what they mean in practice* (2020) by Paul A. Kirschner & Carl Hendrick
- *Principles of Instruction: Research-based strategies that all teachers should know* (2012) by Barak Rosenshine: https://www.teachertoolkit.co.uk/wp-content/uploads/2018/10/Principles-of-Insruction-Rosenshine.pdf

3 Big ideas in science

> In this chapter, we are going to take a look at an important piece of science curriculum thinking: 'big ideas' in science. The concept of these ideas, and the research on which they are based, is something of which you should be aware as a subject leader. We'll go through what they are, how they can inform curriculum thinking and how they can provide coherence to our pupils' learning journey.
>
> Understanding the big ideas in science is the starting point for curriculum design (which is discussed more in the next chapter). You can view them as the end goals of science knowledge for your pupils. As we know, no matter which stage of learning journey you are teaching, we are all working together to help our pupils reach those end goals.

What is a 'big idea'?

'Big ideas' are important and overarching chunks of knowledge in science. They serve as unifying principles that connect and integrate numerous smaller ideas and experiences. A big idea has broad explanatory power, being applicable to a wide range of related events. It serves as a crucial end goal, directing the educational journeys of pupils. These big ideas can also be thought of as threshold concepts.

For example, the knowledge that evolution occurs by natural selection is a big idea. It has huge cultural and historical significance, reflecting a major shift in understanding in the scientific community, promoted by the work of Charles Darwin. It also has broad explanatory power: it is the answer to many questions about the natural world and the diversity found within it. In contrast, the knowledge that the dodo bird is now extinct is a small idea. While it is an interesting and valuable nugget of knowledge, it has a limited application that applies to a specific organism and event. It is not going to answer many other questions about the natural world. It is, however, an important building block of knowledge that could contribute to the understanding of the big idea of evolution.

To grasp a big idea truly, learners must build upon small concepts incrementally throughout their science education, as these notions cannot be taught effectively all at once (Harlen, 2015). Some of these small steps will start in EYFS. For example, for pupils to grasp the concept of evolution, they must first understand the diversity of plants and animals on our planet. This understanding begins in EYFS Early Learning Goals (ELG): The Natural World.

By structuring knowledge around big ideas, we avoid viewing topics as isolated facts; instead, we create an interconnected framework of useful ideas. By organising our curriculums around these central concepts, we encourage our pupils to forge connections between various scientific concepts. This approach not only benefits our pupils: it also challenges us as teachers to prioritise connecting and linking scientific concepts in our planning and teaching.

A big idea in science education can be likened to a keystone in an arch: the arch's most vital stone. It is placed centrally and locks all the other stones into place, providing support for the entire framework of the arch. Similarly, a big idea serves as a central concept that supports the entire framework of knowledge connected beneath it. A big idea provides coherence and structure in the same way that a keystone does.

Smaller ideas and concepts are the building blocks that contribute to the understanding of big ideas. As pupils learn and assimilate these smaller ideas, they provide the necessary foundation and context for comprehending the larger, overarching concepts. Each smaller idea interlocks with the others, forming a network of knowledge that eventually leads to a comprehensive understanding of the big idea.

Without the structure of the smaller ideas, it becomes challenging for learners to grasp and fully appreciate the significance of the big idea. Just as an arch without any of the blocks beneath it would lack stability, the understanding of a big idea without the underlying smaller ideas might be fragmented and incomplete. Figure 3.1 below illustrates an example of how a set of smaller ideas can build towards the understanding of the big idea of evolution by natural selection (represented as the key stone).

In essence, big ideas serve as the keystones of all science education. They offer direction, coherence and depth to the learning experience, while promoting an enriched understanding of the world around us.

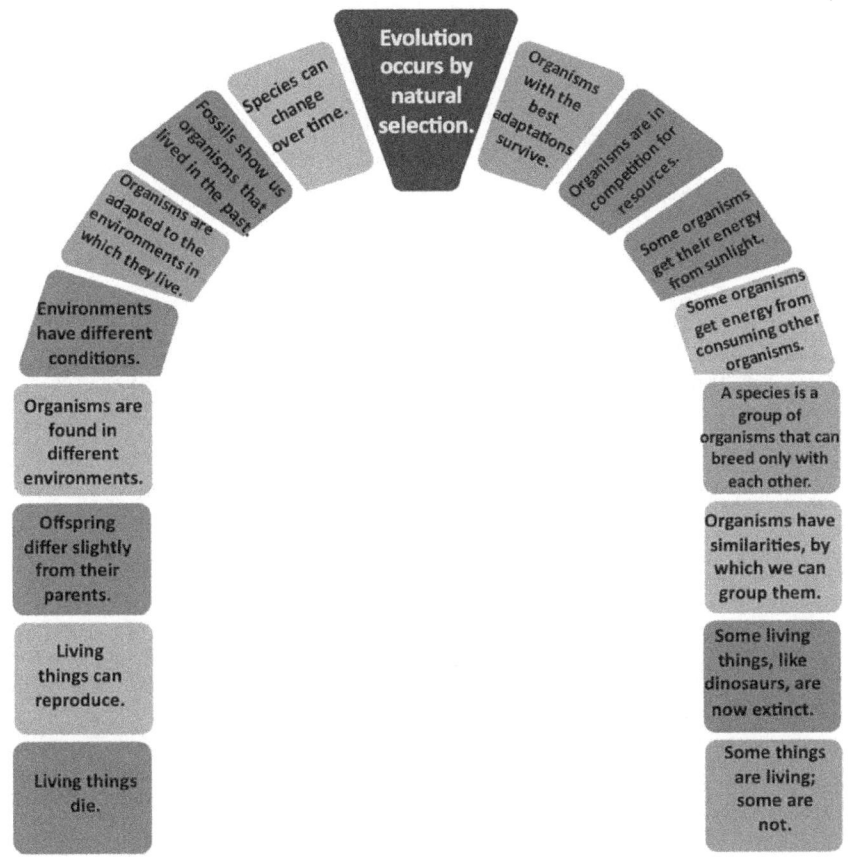

Figure 3.1: The 'keystone' concept of a big idea

What are Harlen's big ideas?

The most well-known and discussed set of big ideas in science comes from a seminar involving ten international experts: a mix of people working in science or science education. The seminar was held with the aim of 'identifying the key ideas that pupils should encounter in their science education to enable them to understand, enjoy and marvel at the natural world'.

The ASE published academic Wynne Harlen's distillation of the conference's discussions, 'Principles and Big Ideas of Science Education' (Harlen, 2010), and a further updated version in 2015.

The criteria for selection of the big ideas were that the idea should:

- have explanatory power in relation to a large number of objects, events and phenomena that are encountered by pupils in their lives during and after their school years
- provide a basis for understanding issues involved in making decisions that affect their own and others' health and wellbeing, the environment and their use of energy
- provide enjoyment and satisfaction in being able to answer or find answers to the kinds of questions that people ask about themselves and the natural world
- have cultural significance (for instance, in affecting views of the human condition), reflecting achievements in the history of science, the inspiration from the study of nature and the impacts of human activity on the environment.

Fourteen ideas were selected: ten 'ideas of science' and four 'ideas about science'. They are as follows.

Ideas *of* science:

1. All material in the Universe is made of very small particles.
2. Objects can affect other objects at a distance.
3. Changing the movement of an object requires a net force to be acting on it.
4. The total amount of energy in the Universe is always the same but energy can be transformed when things change or are made to happen.
5. The composition of the Earth and its atmosphere and the processes occurring within them shape the Earth's surface and its climate.
6. The solar system is a very small part of one of millions of galaxies in the Universe.
7. Organisms are organised on a cellular basis.
8. Organisms require a supply of energy and materials for which they are often dependent on or in competition with other organisms.
9. Genetic information is passed down from one generation of organisms to another.
10. The diversity of organisms, living and extinct, is the result of evolution.

Ideas *about* science:

11. Science assumes that for every effect there is one or more causes.

12. Scientific explanations, theories and models are those that best fit the facts known at a particular time.

13. The knowledge produced by science is used in some technologies to create products to serve human ends.

14. Applications of science often have ethical, social, economic and political implications.

Powerful knowledge

The concept of 'powerful knowledge' overlaps with that of Harlen's big ideas. It is another concept of which you should be aware, as it is often discussed in reference to curriculum planning.

Powerful knowledge in education, as advocated by Michael Young (2014), is specialised, systematic knowledge that enables learners to apply understanding beyond specific contexts. It gives power to pupils, allowing them to think critically, make informed judgments and extend their understanding beyond their everyday experiences. Powerful knowledge is distinct from common-sense knowledge acquired through daily life, as it goes beyond the limited context of one's surroundings: it provides access to deeper insights and broader perspectives.

An example of powerful knowledge in science is an understanding of the fact that all matter is made of very small particles. This fits Young's criteria because it has been discovered by the scientific community, and is not common-sense knowledge. This knowledge is powerful as it has broad explanatory power. It allows pupils to understand multiple science phenomena, such as why different materials have different properties or how chemical reactions can rearrange particles to form new substances.

This example comes from Harlen's list of big ideas, demonstrating the overlap in definitions. The big ideas in science education fall into Young's definition of knowledge that is powerful as they have been chosen for their significance and explanatory power.

All subject leaders need to have a grasp of the powerful knowledge in their subject. Thinking about big ideas and powerful knowledge is the first step in designing a science curriculum. You will be faced with decisions about what knowledge to include in your curriculum, and deciding whether knowledge is powerful is one lens through which to make these decisions.

Schemas

In cognitive science, 'schema' refers to a mental framework, or cognitive structure, that represents organised knowledge about a specific concept, object, event or situation. It is a way our brains organise and categorise information, allowing us to make sense of the world and process new experiences efficiently (Stern, 2019). Schemas are formed through our experiences and learning, and they serve as mental templates. These help us to interpret and understand new information based on our existing knowledge (EEF, 2021).

The big ideas in science education can be used to help pupils build their schemas around topics or ideas. Big ideas represent fundamental and overarching concepts in science, such as evolution, particles, energy or gravity. They help to connect existing information to new information by providing coherence for a set of smaller ideas. These build to enable the understanding of each big idea. The big idea acts as a mental anchor that, in turn, helps pupils connect and make sense of diverse scientific information. As pupils learn about the big ideas, their schemas begin to take shape. As they encounter new information that aligns with the big ideas, their schemas are strengthened and expanded, fostering a deeper comprehension of the subject.

When we encounter new information or experiences, our brains attempt to fit this information into existing schemas. If the new information aligns well, it is easily assimilated and understood. Schemas can then act as cognitive shortcuts by making future recall easier, because whole sets of ideas can be recalled together. This is why prior knowledge helps to build new knowledge. However, if the new information does not fit within any of our existing schemas, we may need to modify them or create new ones to accommodate the novel information.

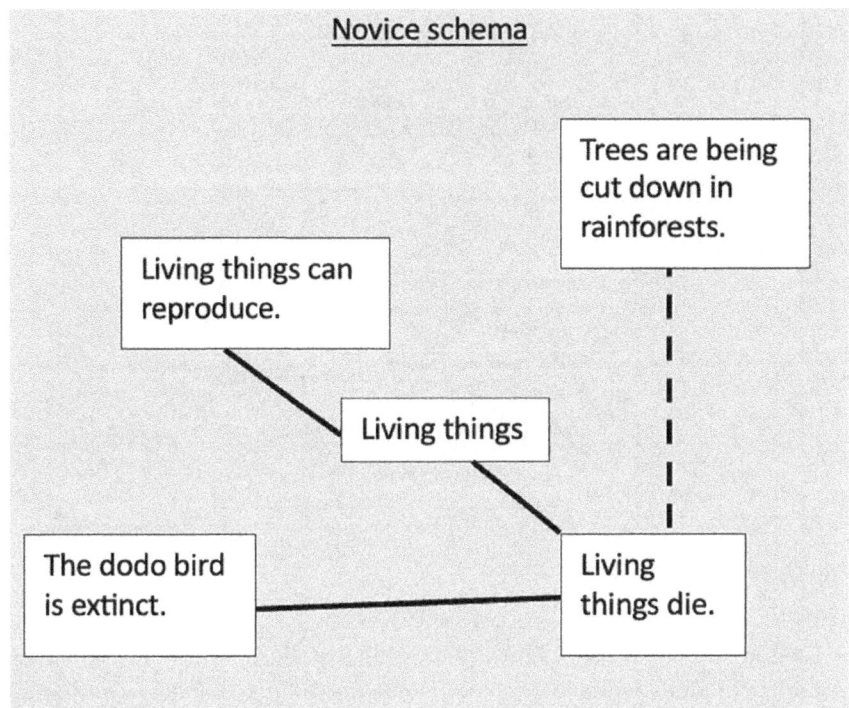

Figure 3.2: An example novice schema

The schema of a novice differs greatly from that of an expert. Novices have less prior knowledge, and their knowledge schemas also tend to be more disorganised as a result: isolated pieces of information may not be well connected. Figure 3.2 illustrates an example of this.

This novice has retained some key science facts in their long-term memory. They know that living things can die and reproduce, but they haven't organised this under the theme of lifecycles. They know that the dodo bird is extinct, and that deforestation is occurring in rainforests, but they lack the knowledge in their schema to link these facts to the concept of diversity or of adaptations. Perhaps their link between living things dying and trees being cut down is also weak because they are not clear that trees are living things.

Imagine that this novice is a Year 6 pupil in your classroom, encountering the big idea of evolution for the first time. You can see that, even if the facts the pupil does have are retrieved, assimilation and complete understanding of the concept of evolution is going to be tricky for them.

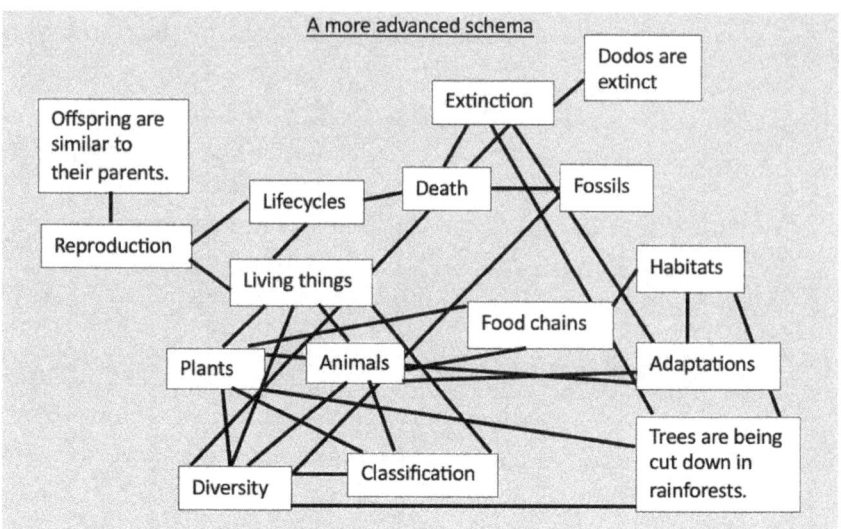

Figure 3.3: *An example expert schema*

On the other hand, experts' schemas are highly organised, with information arranged into meaningful patterns and interconnected networks. Their mental frameworks allow them to access and retrieve relevant information quickly, making their thinking more efficient. A primary-school pupil will never be an expert by the time they leave Year 6 (and even a university degree may not be sufficient for someone to be considered an expert). However, if we think about the journey from novice to expert being a gradient, we can confidently support our pupils to start moving towards the expert end of it.

Figure 3.3 illustrates an example schema of a pupil who is starting to become an expert.

Key facts are organised into topics and can be linked to multiple other topics. If this learner was in your classroom, teaching them about evolution would be an easier task. Once the pupil has grasped that big idea, it will be easier for them to see how it fits with and connects to multiple parts of their schema. This will add an additional layer of organisation, which would aid future problem-solving abilities and science-knowledge acquisition.

So, how can you support your pupils to begin to develop schemas that move them towards the expert end of the gradient? Naturally, you'll need to teach them lots of facts – but you'll also need to make it explicit to them, through modelling and questioning, how their knowledge fits and links together. The examples below illustrate how teachers of different key stages can support their pupils to develop well-linked schemas like the example above.

In practice: developing schemas

Classroom tasks aimed at moving towards expert schemas could look like the examples below.

EYFS: Verbally retrieving prior knowledge and linking to previous learning

Teacher: Today, we're going to read a story about a type of animal called a lizard. Hmmmm we read a story about a different animal last week. Can anyone remember what animal it was?

Pupil: A bear!

Teacher: Great! Look carefully at the lizard on the front cover of my book. How is he different from our bear from last week?

KS1: Making links between learning explicit

Teacher: Can you make a list of all the similarities between plants and animals?

KS2: Visualising how new information links to previous learning

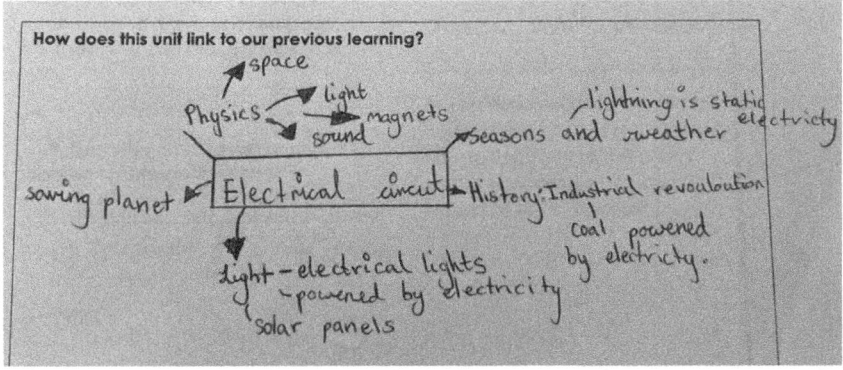

Figure 3.4: How new information links to previous learning

Case study: supporting schema development

Ciaran is a science subject lead at a one-form-entry school in Derbyshire. His school has followed a science scheme of work for the past five years. His teachers like the scheme as it saves them time on planning and, when conducting lesson drop-ins, Ciaran feels that the lessons are high quality.

Ciaran's pupils perform well on the end-of-unit knowledge quizzes provided by the scheme of work. However, when his Year 6 pupils take an old science SAT paper, they score much lower than he expected. The results reveal that many of his pupils are not retaining knowledge from previous years, and are finding it hard to transfer knowledge to unfamiliar contexts.

Ciaran shares his concerns with his line manager, and talks to some of the teachers who also teach science. He realises that the teachers themselves are not clear on what their pupils have learned previously, and how knowledge was being built up in their lessons. They do not appear to be making links between previous units, and they do not understand the importance of this.

Ciaran plans two professional development sessions for teachers. One is on the sequence of knowledge within the science curriculum, so that each teacher is clear on how the smaller ideas in their curriculum are sequenced to enable understanding of bigger ideas. The second is on practical strategies to make these links explicit to pupils in lessons.

Problems with the big ideas

As with any much-discussed concept in educational research, it is important to consider the potential limitations. Harlen's big ideas, whilst the best known, are not the only big ideas in science. Put any ten experts from the field of science in a room, and I am fairly certain the list would differ each time.

One of the criticisms of Harlen's big ideas is that they are incomplete: they do not have enough granularity to organise curriculum content helpfully, particularly within the discipline of chemistry. There is only one of her big ideas that is strictly relevant to chemistry.

This issue has been pointed out by Adam Boxer, who also argues for a missing big idea: surface area to volume ratio. His argument is based on broad explanatory power, as surface area to volume ratio explains, amongst other things:

- adaptations for heat loss
- adaptations for travelling on sand and snow
- structure of cells like the root hair, alveoli or microvilli
- heat loss
- effect of surface area on rates
- nanoparticles' odd properties.

Another example, this time from the discipline of physics, is a change suggested by Jasper Green (2021). In Harlen's list, light and gravity are grouped together because they both act at a distance. Green argues that this is too superficial a similarity, and suggests a different list of physics big ideas. An example from his list is the idea that '[t]he movement of charge forms electric current and causes magnetic fields.'

One of the major problems with Harlen's big ideas, at least as far as the remit of this book is concerned, is that they aren't fully suitable for primary-aged pupils. Many of them contain complex terminology, and the level of understanding required is achievable only once more science has been understood in secondary school.

Harlen attempts to address this by showing the smaller steps needed to build each big idea from primary age levels. She looks, for example, at this big idea: 'The total amount of energy in the Universe is always the same but can be transferred from one energy store to another during an event'. Harlen describes the starting point for this knowledge being that '[t]here are various ways of causing an event or bringing about change in objects and materials'.

Even with suggestions about progression given, it could still be argued that a separate set of ideas aimed at primary level could be created. These would be much more usable by primary pupils, teachers and leaders. So don't worry, I've done exactly that, so you don't have to! In the next section, we'll take a look at my primary-friendly version of the big ideas. It could be used as a starting point for planning a primary science curriculum, which we will explore further in the next chapter.

The big ideas in primary science

So, what could a list of primary-appropriate big ideas look like? Here are my suggestions, along with some of their constituent smaller ideas. The table also includes links with EYFS statutory guidance and topics for Key Stages 1 and 2 in the National Curriculum for England. (The recommendations come with the caveat, of course, that a different scientist might come up with a different list!)

DISCIPLINE	BIG IDEAS*	SOME SMALLER IDEAS	EYFS STATUTORY GUIDANCE LINKS	KS1 AND KS2 CURRICULUM LINKS
Biology	1: Organisms are made up of different parts, which each has a different function.	• Defining living things • What living things need • Parts and functions of plants • Parts and functions of humans	• The Natural World	• Plants • Animals, including humans • Living things and their habitats
	2: Every organism has a life cycle, which includes reproduction resulting in offspring that are similar to their parents.	• Life cycles of different plants and animals • Growth and development • Reproduction	• The Natural World	• Plants • Animals, including humans • Living things and their habitats
	3: An ecosystem is a community of organisms interacting with each other and their physical environment.	• Habitats • Food chains • Predators, prey, producers and consumers • Environmental pressures	• The Natural World	• Plants • Animals, including humans • Living things and their habitats
	4: The diversity of organisms, living and extinct, is the result of evolution by natural selection.	• Classification • Habitats • Adaptations	• The Natural World	• Plants • Animals, including humans • Living things and their habitats • Rocks • Evolution and inheritance
Chemistry	5: Objects are made from materials; materials are made from at least one substance.	• Differences between objects and materials • Properties of materials • Natural materials • How synthetic materials are made • Choosing the correct materials • Differences between pure substances and mixtures	• Creating with Materials	• Everyday materials • States of matter • Properties and changes of materials

DISCIPLINE	BIG IDEAS*	SOME SMALLER IDEAS	EYFS STATUTORY GUIDANCE LINKS	KS1 AND KS2 CURRICULUM LINKS
	6: Changes to substances can be chemical or physical, but mass is always conserved.	• Mixing • Dissolving and solutions • Reversible and irreversible changes • Changes of state • Chemical reactions • Reactivity • Separating mixtures	• The Natural World • Creating with Materials	• Everyday materials • States of matter • Properties and changes of materials
	7: Everything is made of particles; the behaviour and arrangement of particles explain the properties of different substances.	• Properties of materials • Properties of solids, liquids and gases • Particle arrangements in solids, liquids and gases • Effects of heat on particles • Differences between pure substances and mixtures	• Creating with Materials	• Everyday materials • States of matter • Properties and changes of materials
	8: The structure and position of Earth is responsible for changes to climate, land and water.	• The structure of Earth • Rocks and the rock cycle • Soil • Weathering • Tectonic plates • The water cycle	• The Natural World	• Seasonal changes • Rocks • States of matter • Earth and space
Physics	9: Earth is a planet orbiting our Sun, which is one of many stars in our galaxy.	• Earth and the Sun • Axis rotation and orbit • The Moon • Stars and constellations • Planets		• Earth and space • Forces
	10: Every particle in our universe attracts every other particle with a gravitational force.	• Forces: pushes and pulls • Particle arrangements in solids, liquids and gases • Gravity • Orbits		• Forces
	11: Objects interact with each other, giving rise to pairs of forces; imbalance in these can change the sizes and/or movements of objects	• Forces: pushes and pulls • Floating and sinking • Friction • Gravity • Air and water resistance • Levers, pulleys and gears		• Forces and magnets • Forces
	12: The movement of charge forms electric current and causes magnetic fields.	• Static electricity • Electrical circuits • Magnetic and non-magnetic materials • Poles of a magnet • Compasses • Magnetic fields		• Forces and magnets • Electricity

DISCIPLINE	BIG IDEAS*	SOME SMALLER IDEAS	EYFS STATUTORY GUIDANCE LINKS	KS1 AND KS2 CURRICULUM LINKS
	13: Some objects emit light and some sound; both sound and light can travel through different substances and be detected, allowing us to see and hear	• Light sources • How we see • Shadows • Reflection • Sound production and vibration • How we hear • Volume • Pitch		• Light • Sound

*Adapted from Harlen (2010), Jasper Green (2021) and Charles Tracy (2018).

Chapter summary

- Harlen's big ideas were part of a seminal publication that has been much discussed by science leaders and teachers since its release.
- Similar thinking has been done across the field of education, such as Michael Young's on powerful knowledge.
- The big ideas of science can be considered as the end goals of science knowledge that we want our pupils to grasp.
- They can function as a lens through which curriculum thinking can be organised.
- Using big ideas to organise thinking can help pupils to create strong, lasting mental schemas of knowledge.
- This can provide coherence and a deeper level of understanding for key science topics, for both learners and teachers.

Questions for reflection

- Does our science curriculum ensure our pupils have a secure understanding of the big ideas in science?
- Are the big ideas a useful tool for organising our curriculum? How do they help to organise knowledge in pupils' minds?
- What have my pupils learned before each lesson that will help them to understand it?

- Before teaching a science lesson, do science teachers think about how the content fits into pupils' overall learning journey?

Example PD session: drawing on prior knowledge

Here is an example of what a PD session on utilising pupils' prior knowledge could look like.

TIMING SUGGESTION	SESSION GUIDANCE
10 mins	Use the 'What is a 'big idea'?' and 'Schemas' sections of this chapter to explain the concept of big ideas, and their importance in building schemas.
10 mins	Ask teachers to sort a list of smaller ideas into the fields of big ideas in your science curriculum.
10 mins	• Give teachers time to reflect on their learning objectives for upcoming lessons. • Discuss what relevant prior knowledge their pupils should retrieve for each.
15 mins	• Give teachers the opportunity to script how they will introduce the links to prior learning in their upcoming lessons, and what retrieval questions they will ask. • Ask teachers to rehearse their scripts together, with opportunity for peer feedback.

Explore further

- The ASE's *Principles and Big Ideas of Science Education* (2010) https://www.ase.org.uk/bigideas
- The EEF's *Cognitive Science Approaches in the Classroom: A review of the evidence* (2021) (see 'Working with schemas') by Perry et al.
- TheScienceTeacher.co.uk's *Science teaching resources and pedagogy: Challenge your students to make meaning in science*: https://thescienceteacher.co.uk/

4 Curriculum design principles

As a subject lead, one of your most crucial tasks is designing an effective curriculum. But what exactly is a curriculum, and what factors should you consider when creating one?

In this chapter, we'll explore the answers to these questions. We'll look at good principles of curriculum design (or curriculum planning - we'll use both terms throughout), and how to apply them to create a rich, challenging science curriculum that forms coherent threads across year groups.

As a subject lead, your task is to navigate these complexities, making informed choices that will shape the scientific education of your pupils. While it may seem daunting, remember that a well-designed curriculum has the power to inspire curiosity, foster critical thinking and lay the foundation for a lifelong engagement with science.

Whether you are designing a curriculum from scratch or auditing an existing one, this chapter will lay out the key principles of curriculum design to consider.

What is a curriculum?

A curriculum sets out what we want pupils to learn. You are likely to be familiar with the catch-phrase 'Intent, Implementation and Impact' with regards to curriculum planning, and unpicking these terms can provide a useful frame for articulating the curriculum.

- **Intent** is what you intend to teach. What are the topics, ideas and concepts that you want pupils to learn? To determine this, you will draw on your knowledge of the subject alongside your knowledge of your pupils and school context. This should be mapped out and sequenced into a top-level overview.

- **Implementation** is *how* teachers will teach the curriculum. It includes both subject-specific pedagogy and resources such as the schemes, lesson plans, worksheets, slideshows, planned explanations, expositions and questions. Implementation is how the curriculum comes to life. It is how plans translate into classroom practice, and relates directly to the pupils' actual experience of the curriculum. This will be discussed further in Chapters 7–10.
- **Impact** is the learning that results from the curriculum. This will be covered in more detail in Chapter 6.

Planning the curriculum begins with intent. This chapter explores your role in overseeing what will be taught, and sequencing knowledge to build pupil learning.

Going deeper, curriculum is about the choices we make regarding what to teach our students and why those choices matter. Every time we choose to include something, we're also choosing not to include many other possibilities. This responsibility can be daunting, as our choices are always open to debate. Nevertheless, these choices must be made.

Using schemes of work

Many schools will use schemes of work that have been developed by external organisations. These can be great starting points for curriculum and planning resources, can save time and can support with any lack of subject expertise. Even if your school is using a scheme of work it is still important that as a subject leader you are clear on what the principles of effective curriculum planning are. This will enable you to tailor, improve and evaluate any schemes of work that you are currently using or may be looking to use in the future.

It is important that no scheme should ever be static: it should be a fluid entity, responding to the needs of your pupils. It's also vital to note that a scheme of work is not a curriculum: it is just one way of enacting a curriculum. We can use them to guide us, but we should always be clear how they fit into our wider curriculum aims. The next chapter will take you through the steps of planning a curriculum; even if you're using a scheme of work, I suggest reading through those steps so you have a clear understanding of where your scheme can fit into the wider curriculum.

'Twin sins' of curriculum design

Grant Wiggins and Jay McTighe (2005) identified two common mistakes in curriculum design, which they term the 'twin sins':

- Activity-based design: This approach engages pupils with hands-on learning, but lacks academic rigour and fails to consider the broader learning journey. The activity becomes the learning, rather than being a means to it.
- Coverage-focused design: This occurs when teachers rush through content to meet external requirements, resulting in only surface-level learning. Cognitive scientist Daniel Willingham notes that this leads to shallow knowledge: pupils having some understanding, but not being able to transfer or apply it effectively (Willingham, 2009).

As a subject lead who's embarking on designing a science curriculum, you may find it helpful to bear these twin sins in mind.

Guiding principles of curriculum design

As well as being aware of some common pitfalls, it is also helpful to have a set of guiding principles in mind. Wiliam (2013) sets out seven principles of good curriculum design.

A CURRICULUM MUST BE…	IT SHOULD…
balanced	promote intellectual, moral, spiritual, aesthetic, creative, emotional and physical development as being equally important
rigorous	seek to develop intra-disciplinary habits of mind, teaching the subject matter in a way that is faithful to its discipline
coherent	make explicit links between the different topics and experiences encountered
vertically integrated	focus on progression by carefully sequencing knowledge and providing clarity about what it means to get better at the subject

A CURRICULUM MUST BE…	IT SHOULD…
appropriate	look to avoid making unreasonable demands by matching the level of challenge to a pupil's current level of maturity and knowledge
focused	seek to keep the curriculum manageable by identifying big ideas or key concepts and teaching the most important knowledge
relevant	seek to connect the valued outcomes of a curriculum to the pupils being taught, providing opportunities for pupils to make informed choices.

The aims of a curriculum

The first step in curriculum design is laying out your aims. What is it you want your curriculum to achieve? A good starting point for this is your national curriculum. The main aims for science in the National Curriculum for England are to ensure that all pupils:

- develop scientific knowledge and conceptual understanding through the specific disciplines of biology, chemistry and physics
- develop understanding of the nature, processes and methods of science, through different types of science enquiries that help them to answer scientific questions about the world around them
- are equipped with the scientific knowledge required to understand the uses and implications of science, today and for the future.

Subject leads should not feel restricted to these aims, though: they can be seen as a guide. Many school curriculums will encompass them, but curriculum designs are likely to go beyond them to meet the overarching values and aims of the school.

It's also important to bear in mind that there are always trade-offs. As a science lead, you will need to consider carefully what to emphasise in your curriculum – and, as a result, what you may need to leave out. For example, will you spend content time covering a range of scientific careers, or on ensuring all pupils frequently take part in group work?

Case study: reviewing a curriculum

Karen joins a new school, and is asked to take on the role of science subject lead. She decides to start by reviewing the current curriculum.

The school has always used the same scheme of work. However, when Karen speaks to teachers about it, they aren't very positive. It seems that most of them spend quite a lot of time replanning the lessons so that the content is more suitable for their classes. When Karen reviews the scheme, she also finds it unclear regarding how substantive and disciplinary knowledge are broken down, and how pupils progress.

Karen decides to change the scheme they are using, and see if they can find one that is higher quality and better suited to their context. She starts by writing a set of aims for the new intended science curriculum, aligning them with the whole-school values of academic excellence, kindness and celebrating diversity.

Karen explores whether each scheme of work she reviews meets these aims, and also whether it stands up to the principles of good curriculum design. One scheme fits all these requirements other than featuring a diverse range of scientists. Karen decides to go ahead with the scheme of work, but plans to match each unit with a story that displays a wider range of diversity in scientists.

Once Karen has chosen the scheme, she shares it with colleagues to gauge their opinions. She also asks an experienced teacher to trial the lesson plans for a half term. The feedback from her colleagues and the teacher trialling the resources is positive, so Karen decides to formalise the change to the new scheme and introduce it to the rest of the teaching staff.

Substantive and disciplinary knowledge

In designing an effective science curriculum, it's crucial to understand and incorporate both substantive and disciplinary knowledge. These two forms of knowledge are fundamental to building scientific expertise: they ensure that pupils not only know scientific facts but also understand how scientific knowledge is generated and revised.

Substantive knowledge involves:

- the 'products' or 'facts' of science
- established concepts, laws, theories and models
- what we typically think of as scientific content knowledge.

Disciplinary knowledge consists of understanding:

- the methods and practices of science
- the ways in which scientific knowledge is generated, validated and revised over time
- various types of scientific enquiry.

For example, substantive knowledge is understanding that all living organisms reproduce. Disciplinary knowledge is understanding that scientists usually make predictions before they do experiments.

High-quality science curriculums carefully sequence both substantive and disciplinary knowledge: it's crucial to avoid teaching them separately. Instead, embedding disciplinary knowledge within the substantive content of biology, chemistry and physics provides a more accurate representation of how science works. As pupils progress through the curriculum, they should build connected knowledge of both scientific concepts and procedures. This enables them to reason scientifically about phenomena with increasing sophistication, and to work scientifically with growing expertise.

In the National Curriculum for England, substantive knowledge corresponds to the 'knowledge' statements, and disciplinary knowledge aligns with the 'working scientifically' statements.

The importance of careful sequencing

Careful sequencing is a critical aspect of effective curriculum design. This is particularly true for science, where knowledge is often hierarchical in nature. When teachers become skilled curriculum-makers, they plan the sequence of each element meticulously, unlocking and making accessible even the most complex and ambitious content. This deliberate journey towards connectedness forms what is often referred to as the 'intended curriculum'.

The purpose of this careful sequencing is to guide pupils from being novices within their subject domains to becoming more expert – concepts we explored in the 'Schemas' section of Chapter 3. Pupils' understanding may initially be shallow but, through gradual and progressive learning over time, more connections are made. These connections occur both internally as pupils' schemas become more sophisticated, and explicitly within the structure of what is taught: the curriculum. This approach helps to deepen understanding: pupils not only know more but can also see the links between what they already know and their new learning.

Coherent curriculum design should therefore be viewed as a whole-school enterprise, embodying the concept that it forms a progression model. This model should be both overarching and detailed: progress shouldn't be seen as ticking off vague descriptors, but instead ensuring children have remembered the concepts, content and skills set out. We need to think about a pupil's journey through the whole curriculum, not just the term or year they are currently in.

In this model of progression, pupils remember what they need to know from previous years and use it to make sense of what they learn in coming years, continually deepening their understanding. Over time, certain aspects become effortless, becoming an automatic part of pupils' thinking apparatus. As a primary science lead, your role here is crucially important. Individual teachers are responsible for only their section of the curriculum journey – but, as a subject lead, you have the oversight to ensure coherence from teacher to teacher.

In practice: sequencing a science topic

A whole-school plan for the careful sequencing of the physics topic 'light' could look like the example below. In order to provide context, it includes pre-EYFS and secondary-level aims around those for primary school.

STAGE	PUPILS SHOULD BE ABLE TO…
Before EYFS	• repeat actions that have an effect
EYFS	• explore how things work • talk about differences in materials and changes they notice • describe what they see, hear and feel whilst outside
KS1	• identify, name, draw and label the basic parts of the human body • say which part of the body is associated with each sense • describe the simple physical properties of a variety of everyday materials

STAGE	PUPILS SHOULD BE ABLE TO…
Lower KS2	• recognise that they need light in order to see things and that dark is the absence of light • notice that light is reflected from surfaces • recognise that light from the Sun can be dangerous and that there are ways to protect their eyes • recognise that shadows are formed when the light from a light source is blocked by an opaque object • find patterns in the way that the size of a shadow changes
Upper KS2	• compare and group together everyday materials on the basis of their properties, including their hardness, solubility, transparency, conductivity (electrical and thermal), and response to magnets • recognise that light appears to travel in straight lines • use the idea that light travels in straight lines to explain that objects are seen because they give out or reflect light into the eye • explain that we see things because light travels from light sources to our eyes or from light sources to objects and then to our eyes • use the idea that light travels in straight lines to explain why shadows have the same shapes as the objects that cast them
KS3	• understand the similarities and differences between light waves and waves in matter • describe how light waves travel through a vacuum • know the speed of light • understand how light is transmitted through materials: absorption, diffuse scattering and specular reflection at a surface • use a ray model to explain imaging in mirrors, the pinhole camera and the refraction of light, and to explain the action of a convex lens in focusing (qualitative), including in the human eye • understand how light transfers energy from source to absorber, leading to chemical and electrical effects, and photo-sensitive material in retinas and cameras • comprehend the nature of colours and the different frequencies of light, white light and prisms (qualitative), and the differential colour effects in absorption and diffuse reflection

By starting curriculum planning with the end in mind, and carefully sequencing content, we can create a complex web of interconnected knowledge: a schema for our pupils. This approach gives them every opportunity to extend and connect what they know in meaningful ways. It can prepare their memories for incoming information by providing a structure into which new information can be integrated. Without this careful sequencing, we risk leaving pupils with gaps in their understanding as they tackle more-challenging work moving through school.

As Christine Counsell (2018) eloquently puts it, 'curriculum is content structured as narrative over time'. This narrative approach, built on meticulous sequencing, is especially crucial in science education, where a secure understanding of each key block of knowledge is often necessary before progression to the next stage. By focusing on careful sequencing, we can create clearer connections between different topics, reduce the cognitive load on pupils, and ultimately foster more-effective learning.

The need for detail

Breaking down curriculum content into specified, granular detail is a crucial aspect of effective curriculum planning. Having a curriculum that specifies learning intricately is important for many reasons.

- It avoids unintended repetition: clear specification guards against the same content being taught at the same level of complexity multiple times across different year groups.
- It provides clarity for teachers: offering a clear overview of precise knowledge frees teachers from content determination, allowing them to focus on effective teaching strategies, adaptations and identification of areas for further challenge or support.
- It aligns with principles of cognitive science: breaking knowledge into small steps helps manage cognitive load, as noted in Rosenshine's 'Principles of Instruction' (2012).
- It supports clear progression: sequencing knowledge effectively builds a curriculum in which each concept is broken down into manageable units to be mastered.
- It overcomes the 'curse of knowledge': it helps experts better understand and communicate complex topics from a novice's perspective.

- It enables precise retrieval practice: scope for more-specific and effective questioning enhances long-term memory through targeted recall of previously learned information.
- It facilitates curriculum refinement: identifying and adding absent essential knowledge into previous year groups ensures a coherent and comprehensive learning journey.

Chapter summary

- Curriculum design is a complex process that involves carefully selecting and sequencing content to create a coherent learning journey for pupils.
- Breaking down curriculum content into specific, granular detail is crucial for avoiding repetition, providing clarity for teachers and aligning with principles of cognitive science.
- Careful sequencing of curriculum content supports the development of deep knowledge, and helps pupils progress from novice to expert understanding.
- Both substantive knowledge (facts, concepts and theories) and disciplinary knowledge (scientific practices and methods) are essential components of a well-designed science curriculum.
- Integrating substantive and disciplinary knowledge, rather than teaching them separately, provides a more authentic representation of how science works.

Questions for reflection

- How does our current science curriculum balance substantive and disciplinary knowledge?
- In what ways does our curriculum break down complex scientific concepts into smaller, more-manageable units of knowledge?
- How does our curriculum support the progression of pupils' understanding from novice to expert?
- To what extent does our current curriculum facilitate retrieval practice? How might we incorporate more opportunities for retrieval throughout the curriculum?

- In what ways does our curriculum design process allow for ongoing refinement and improvement? How might we make this process more systematic and responsive to pupil needs?

Example PD session: incorporating medium-term curriculum plans into lesson design

Here is an example of what a PD session on aligning teaching with medium-term curriculum plans could look like.

TIMING SUGGESTION	SESSION GUIDANCE
5 mins	Elicit input from teachers on the different levels of the curriculum, starting with its overall aims. Include its medium- and long-term plans, discussing sequencing and mapping.
10 mins	Model how to plan a great science lesson from the medium-term planning that is available to teachers.
15 mins	Ask teachers to spend time planning a science lesson based on your model and the curriculum's medium-term plan.
15 mins	Prompt teachers, in pairs, to discuss and refine their plans with one another before feeding back to the group.

Explore further

- Neil Almond's blog *Ramble #6: Achieving coherence in primary science (Why primary science needs to be less like the Simpsons and more like Game of Thrones)*: https://nutsaboutteaching.wordpress.com/2019/01/04/ramble-6-achieving-coherence-in-primary-science-why-primary-science-needs-to-be-less-like-the-simpsons-and-more-like-game-of-thrones/
- *Curriculum: Theory, Culture and the Subject Specialisms* (2021) by Ruth Ashbee
- *Primary Huh: curriculum conversations with subject leaders in primary schools* (2022) by Mary Myatt and John Tomsett

- *The researchED guide to The Curriculum: An evidence-informed guide for teachers* (2020), edited by Clare Sealy
- researchEDHome 2020's video *Jon Hutchinson: Seven Distinctions Every Subject Leader Should Know About*: https://www.youtube.com/watch?v=RAhVhlaNQlc

5 How to plan a curriculum

> This chapter is laid out slightly differently from the other chapters. It builds directly on the last one, on the principles of effective curriculum design, and lays out a step-by-step process through which a subject leader may plan a science curriculum. It can be used as a 'how to' guide if you are starting from scratch or, if you're reviewing only an aspect of your curriculum, each section could be read in isolation as a refresher. The steps in the process are:
>
> 1. Laying out the aims of the curriculum
> 2. Starting at the end
> 3. Mapping progression of substantive and disciplinary knowledge
> 4. Creating long-term plans
> 5. Mapping additional key features
> 6. Creating medium-term plans

Step 1: Laying out the aims of the curriculum

As mentioned in the previous chapter, the first step of planning any curriculum is to lay out its aims. Your national curriculum, and your school values and vision, are good places to start.

In practice: a vision for primary science

Aims of a primary science curriculum could look like the examples below.
- Give pupils the knowledge they need to live healthy and fulfilled lives.
- Create citizens who make positive contributions to the future of our planet and society.
- Inspire the next generation of science leaders.
- Teach that everyone can be a scientist.
- Teach in a way that fosters curiosity and lifelong love for the subject.

- Teach scientific skills explicitly, providing lots of opportunity for practical, hands-on experience.
- Impart the knowledge needed for pupils to make sense of, and revel in, the world around them.

Step 2: Starting at the end

The next step is to start with the end points. You need to be clear about what it is you want pupils to have learned by the end of their curriculum journey with you, which, unless you work in an all-through school, will be Year 6 for most. Of course, your national curriculum is again a great starting point as it lays out end-of-key-stage expectations. However, a great curriculum thinker will go further than this.

Subject associations can be good sources of advice. You could also speak to colleagues who teach Key Stage 3 about what they consider the most-important threshold concepts for pupils to have grasped before starting their Key Stage 3 curriculums. Chapter 3, on 'big ideas' in science, is also relevant: these are concepts that have been identified by experts as the most important, powerful and relevant science knowledge for pupils to grasp.

It is equally important that you lay out the end points for both substantive and disciplinary knowledge. You should make it clear what methods and approaches pupils should have learned at the end of your curriculum, as well as what information they are expected to know.

In practice: the end point for primary science in Y6

End points for a primary science curriculum could look like the examples below.

Pupils should:

- have secure knowledge of the topics in our national curriculum
- be able to conduct scientific enquiries
- be able write up investigation reports for scientific enquiries
- have secure knowledge of the 'big ideas' of science.

Sourcing or producing model examples of work can be a useful part of refining your aims. For example, what does a model investigation report look like? What is an example of a piece of work that shows secure understanding of the curriculum topic of light? You will want to ensure that end points are not vague, and that teachers know exactly what they are working towards.

Step 3: Mapping progression of substantive and disciplinary knowledge

Once the curriculum end points have been decided, your next task is to work backwards: you need to break down the end points into detailed descriptions of the knowledge the curriculum should include. This is often referred to as 'backwards planning', an approach advocated by Wiggins and McTighe (2005). This backwards planning needs to be done for both substantive and disciplinary knowledge.

This is a large but necessary piece of work. For example, if you've included the end point that pupils should have secure knowledge of the topics in your national curriculum, you need to map the progression of knowledge for every one of those topics. This may seem like a daunting task, but there are resources out there to help (some of which are free, and suggested in the 'Explore further' section at the end of this chapter).

Lots of this mapping is also done within national curriculums themselves. The National Curriculum for England contains, for example, statements of progression ready for 'working scientifically'. The Scottish Curriculum of Excellence has this approach mapped out as 'inquiry and investigative skills'.

It can be useful, in addition, to include what pupils will learn after their primary learning journey, to think about how concepts build between Upper Key Stage 2 and Key Stage 3. This is not strictly necessary for a primary science lead, but there are again resources that can help. The PLAN assessment resources are particularly useful here, as they include Key Stage 3 in all their unit-progression documents.

In practice: backwards-planning for the topic of cells

Granular objectives for the topic of cells could look like the examples below.

Year 1 Unit: The animal kingdom
- Learn 'MRS GREN' for identification of living things: all living things Move, Reproduce, Sense, Grow, Respire, Excrete and (require) Nutrition.
Year 4 Unit: Human anatomy

- Learn what a cell is, and a few examples (e.g. red blood cells).
- Learn that the body is made of organ systems that carry out different bodily functions.

Year 6 Unit: Humans and animals over time

- Learn about classification and the five 'kingdoms': plants, animals, fungi, protists and prokaryotes.
- Learn that protists and prokaryotes are single-celled organisms.

Year 7 Unit: Cells

- Learn about animal and plant cells, and the differences and similarities between the structures of cells.
- Learn how to identify the different organelles and their roles.

Year 7 Unit: Cell structures

- Learn about cells' structures and their functions.
- Learn about how molecules move by diffusion.

Year 8 Unit: Specialised cells

- Learn about how cells adapt to different functions by altering shape.

In practice: backwards-planning writing reports

A plan for the granular skills of writing investigation reports could look like the example below.

Years	ELEMENTS OF A SCIENTIFIC WRITE-UP				
	Variables	Diagrams	Method	Results	Conclusion
EYFS	Experience investigations (e.g. planting seeds)	See modelled diagrams as investigations are explained	Experience methods being modelled orally	Draw pictures of results	Discuss conclusions orally
Years 1–2	Experience experiments (e.g. growing mould in different conditions)	• Draw parts of partially completed diagrams • Begin to draw own diagrams	• Draw pictures of equipment used • Order the steps of a method	• Fill in results tables • Draw results • Give verbal explanations	• Give verbal explanations • Choose correct conclusion from two options

Years	ELEMENTS OF A SCIENTIFIC WRITE-UP				
	Variables	Diagrams	Method	Results	Conclusion
Years 3–4	• Learn about three types of variable • Identify variables as a class	Draw diagrams using single lines, rulers, pencils, no shading, no colour and labels	Begin to write own methods	Draw own results tables with teacher modelling	Complete conclusions by filling in the gaps (cloze)
Years 5–6	Independently identify variables	Draw diagrams using single lines, rulers, pencils, no shading, no colour and labels	• Write own methods • Begin to plan methods before experiments	Draw own results tables	Begin to complete conclusions independently using the PEE structure

In practice: backwards-planning for the topic of plants (adapted from PLAN progression document)

Granular objectives for the topic of plants could look like the examples below.

Pre-EYFS:

- Use all senses in hands-on exploration of natural materials.
- Plant seeds and care for growing plants.
- Understand the key features of the life cycles of a plant and an animal.

EYFS:

- Use all senses in hands-on exploration of natural materials.
- Describe the plants that they see outside.
- Recognise and describe the effects of changing seasons on the natural world.

Year 1:

- Identify and name a variety of common wild and garden plants, including deciduous and evergreen trees.

- Identify and describe the basic structures of a variety of common flowering plants, including trees.

Year 2:

- Observe and describe how seeds and bulbs grow into mature plants.
- Find out and describe what plants need to stay healthy.
- Identify and name a variety of plants in their habitats.

Year 3:

- Identify and describe the functions of different parts of flowering plants.
- Explore the requirements of plants for life and growth (air, light, water, nutrients from the soil and room to grow), and how they vary from plant to plant.
- Investigate the way in which water is transported within plants.
- Explore the part that flowers play in the life cycle of flowering plants.

Year 4:

- Recognise that living things can be grouped in a variety of ways.
- Explore and use classification keys to help group, identify and name a variety of living things in local and wider environments.
- Recognise that environments can change and that this can sometimes pose dangers to living things.

Year 5:

- Describe the life process of reproduction in some plants.

Year 6:

- Describe how living things are classified into broad groups according to common observable characteristics and based on similarities and differences (including micro-organisms, plants and animals).
- Give reasons for classifying plants and animals based on specific characteristics.

Key Stage 3:

- Describe reproduction in plants, including flower structure, wind and insect pollination, dispersal, fertilisation, and seed and fruit formation.
- Perform quantitative investigations of some dispersal mechanisms.

Step 4: Creating long-term plans

The next step is to create long-term curriculum plans that map when pupils will study which units. You have some choices to make here about how you'll form coherent units from the granular knowledge laid out in previous steps.

There are multiple different ways of doing this. For example, if you have identified that Year 1 pupils need to learn about plants and animals, you might want to create a unit called 'Living things' in which pupils learn about both topics. You might prefer to stick to unit titles that match your national curriculum's unit titles. Alternatively, you might want to organise units by the subject disciplines, and teach a term each of biology, chemistry and physics.

Your school's context is also important. For example, if your school is a coastal one, studying marine ecosystems might feature more heavily in your curriculum. In contrast, an inland rural school might choose to focus on woodland ecosystems. Other things to consider might be scientists famous to your area, resources available to you (such as allotment for plant-growing investigations) or local scientific industries.

When looking at long-term curriculum planning, schools and subject leaders face an important choice between subject-based and topic-based approaches. In a subject-based approach, disciplines are taught discretely: pupils learn science in dedicated science lessons, mathematics in mathematics lessons and so on. Conversely, a topic-based approach integrates multiple subjects under broad themes, such as 'The Ancient World'. While topic-based approaches remain common in UK primary schools, and can cover national-curriculum content, I advise caution with this approach for the following reasons.

Firstly, it can disrupt the logical building of scientific knowledge, as topics might be chosen to fit themes rather than to support understanding. For example, teaching 'States of Matter' alongside *Charlie and the Chocolate Factory* might seem engaging, but the two focuses may not coincide at the right time in pupils' learning journey. The 2021 Ofsted science review also warns against this approach, noting that many curriculums become 'an arbitrary collection of topics introduced in an ad-hoc fashion', making knowledge 'difficult to use and easily forgotten'.

Secondly, this approach can make it harder for pupils to build strong mental schemas of scientific ideas, as their learning becomes scattered across different topics. Thirdly, it risks hiding what makes science special: its unique ways of investigating and understanding the world. This is the disciplinary knowledge of science, which we know should be a large and important part of any curriculum.

Making connections between subjects can enhance learning when they coincide naturally. However, these links shouldn't be at the expense of clear sequencing, coverage and integrity of the discipline of science. The Ofsted review is clear that effective science curriculums are built around 'the logical structure of scientific disciplines' (2021, p. 8). This means teaching science in a way that helps pupils to see how different scientific ideas connect and build upon each other. When pupils can see these connections in science clearly, they're much more likely to develop deep, lasting scientific understanding that they can use and apply in the future. It is important for pupils to know that they are learning science, and to be clear on the knowledge and skills that scientists need. While this could still be achieved through topic-based teaching, subject-specific teaching by its very nature makes it easier to achieve.

(Examples of long-term science curriculum plans can be found via the suggestions in the 'Primary education sources and guidance' section of Chapter 2.)

Step 5: Mapping additional key features

Once units have been mapped out in long-term plans, it is important for you to consider and map out other key elements of the curriculum. Some elements you might want to consider planning out include:

- vocabulary and key definitions
- the types of equipment pupils will use

- the types of enquiry in which pupils will take part
- which scientists and scientific careers pupils will investigate
- which trips will accompany which units
- research projects in which pupils could take part
- any stories that may naturally complement the unit.

Planning out these elements at this stage ensures you have good coverage, and that teachers are provided with a high level of detail. For example, by mapping out which scientists pupils will encounter in the curriculum, you can ensure that pupils are exposed to a diverse range of scientists. By mapping out key vocabulary for each year group, you can ensure key terms are being used consistently, and that teachers have a clear record of what terms should be included in retrieval practice at any given point. This approach will also ensure you can source or create resources efficiently.

Essentially, any element that you think is important in your curriculum should be mapped out at this stage. If, later down the line, you want to add something you haven't mapped (for example, scientists pupils encounter incidentally), you can adapt your plans. This will impact other considerations, however: for example, resources that have already been created may need to change.

Step 6: Creating medium-term plans

This next step takes us to a point somewhere between the 'macro' level of curriculum aims and the 'micro' level of granular backwards-planning. Medium-term plans are the maps at which teachers will look before starting to teach their next units. Sometimes medium-term planning is completed by the subject lead; sometimes it is completed by teachers, with subject leads' guidance and support.

In each unit's medium-term plan, it should be clear:

- what the key substantive knowledge of the unit is
- what the key disciplinary knowledge of the unit is
- how learning progresses across each lesson of the unit

- how new learning builds on previous learning
- what enquiry types the unit will include (if appropriate)
- what the end point and/or end assessment of the unit will be.

In practice: a medium-term plan

A medium-term for the Year 4 topic 'Adaptation' may look like the example below.

YEAR 4: SPRING TERM	
Unit Title: Adaptation	**Unit Length:** 6 weeks
Key concepts: • Organisms' requirements for energy • Genetic information • Evolution	
Relevant end points covered: A) Students understand the key concepts of the curriculum. C) Students can ask questions and make observations about the world around them using scientific knowledge. E) Students understand some of the major issues facing our planet and have an appreciation of the importance of science to wider society.	
Possible misconceptions: • Pupils may misunderstand the relationship between food and energy. • Pupils may believe that: • camels' humps store water • cacti have no leaves • all ocean creatures are 'fish', including whales and dolphins • only large animals are consumers • an organism higher on a food chain is a predator of all the organisms below • individuals can adapt to change in the environment if they need to.	
Previous learning: • The Animal Kingdom (Year 1) • Plants (Year 1) • Habitats (Year 2)	**Assessments:** End-of-topic quiz
Extra-curricular activities: Trip to WWF centre	**Cross-curricular links:** • Temperatures (maths) • Scales (maths)

> **Level 1 core knowledge:**
> Pupils understand:
> - the fact that different organisms get their energy from different sources
> - the difference between producers and consumers
> - the fact that food chains show the flow of energy between organisms, with the direction of arrows showing energy transfer
> - how to interpret and label food chains
> - how to construct food chains.
>
> **Level 2 core knowledge:**
> Pupils understand:
> - the definition of 'environment'
> - the key characteristics of desert, arctic and underwater environments
> - interlinks between definitions of 'habitat', 'environment' and 'ecosystem' (for example, that an ecosystem can contain more than one environment, like the environments above and below the ice in the arctic).

Knowledge organisers

Some schools create 'knowledge organisers' that map out all the key knowledge that pupils are expected to learn for each unit. These are structured documents that distil the essential knowledge, vocabulary and skills pupils need to master within a specific topic or unit. Subject leaders may find them a helpful medium-term planning tool because they make sure all teachers cover the same key content, and also help new teachers to see exactly what needs to be taught. They can also be used by pupils in lessons as reference guides, to support quizzing and for communicating a curriculum to parents and carers.

However, knowledge organisers do have some downsides: they can make complicated topics seem too simple, and might not show all the different ways pupils need to think about and use their learning. They can also be very time-consuming to make. It is up to you, as a subject lead, whether you want to use them as a part of your medium-term planning.

In practice: a knowledge organiser

Figure 5.1 below illustrates an example knowledge organiser for the topic 'States of Matter'.

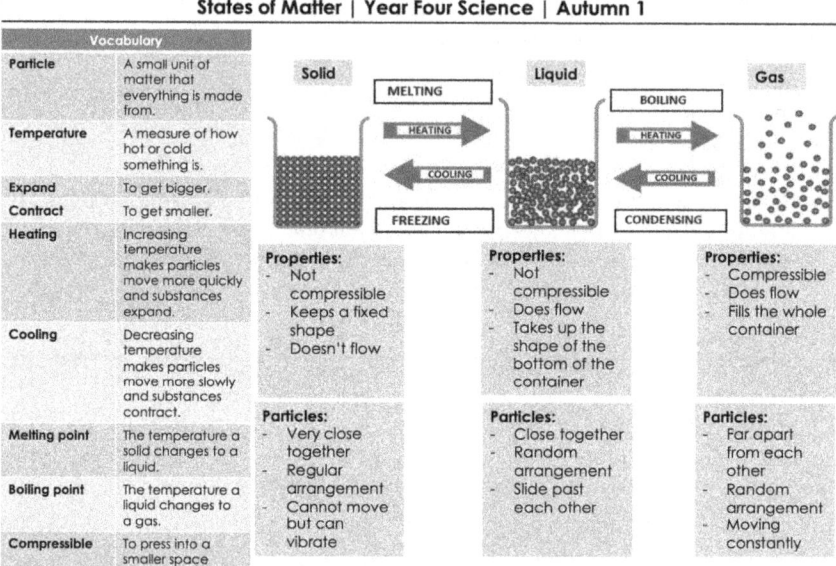

Figure 5.1: A 'States of Matter' knowledge organiser

Explore further

- Chris Fountain's articles and video on how to design a curriculum: https://www.thenational.academy/blog/how-to-design-a-subject-curriculum
- Oak National Academy's curriculum resources for Key Stages 1 and 2 Science: https://www.thenational.academy/teachers/curriculum/science-primary/overview
- The Ogden trust's primary science resources (particularly its explainer sheets for each of the 'working scientifically' strands): https://www.ogdentrust.com/resources/
- PLAN's *Progression in Knowledge, Progression in Vocabulary* and *Working Scientifically Skills*: https://www.planassessment.com/science-subject-leader
- Christopher Such's 'Curriculum Giveaway' documents (which are free to download): https://primarycolour.home.blog/2021/04/07/curriculum-giveaway-2-0-science/

6 Assessment: what do my pupils know?

> Assessment involves gathering information about what our pupils know, interpreting this information and using it for various purposes. This could be, for example, how to plan the next lesson in a series, or to track and communicate progress over time. Assessment can be either formative (conducted before and during instruction, to guide further learning) or summative (conducted to evaluate learning at the end of a period of study).
>
> In this chapter, we explore the key principles of assessment and examine current statutory guidance for science assessment in primary schools. We also look at using both formative and summative assessments to find out what our pupils know at different stages of their learning journeys. Finally, we zoom in on why assessing prior knowledge and misconceptions in science is crucial.

Key principles of assessment

Several key principles, such as the ones below, should underpin effective assessment in primary science.

- **Alignment with curriculum objectives**: Assessments should reflect the full range of learning objectives outlined in your national curriculum, covering both substantive knowledge (content) and disciplinary knowledge (ways of working scientifically).
- **Alignment with purpose**: The purpose of the assessment should guide its design and implementation. Whether it's for formative feedback, summative reporting or accountability, the assessment method should align with its intended use (Nuffield, 2012).
- **Integration with teaching**: Assessment should be an integral part of the teaching process, enabling pupils to understand the purposes of their activities and improving the quality of their work.

- **Multiple methods**: Effective assessment combines qualitative and quantitative data from various individual and group-learning activities.
- **Manageability**: Assessment procedures should be realistic and manageable for both pupils and teachers, with transparent time demands. Teacher workload should be considered.
- **Effectiveness of feedback**: Assessment should provide constructive guidance to learners about how to improve, developing their capacity for self-assessment and reflective learning (Wiliam, 2014).

Reliability and validity

Think of assessment like a measuring tool: we need to trust that it works properly every time we use it. Two key questions help us determine if our assessment is working well:

1. Does it give us consistent results? This is what we call reliability.
2. Does it actually measure what we want it to measure? This is what we call validity.

Let's talk about consistency first. A good assessment should work like a reliable bathroom scale: if you weigh yourself three times in a row, the scales should show roughly the same number every time. Several factors can affect how reliable our assessments are. These include:

- the types of questions we use (such as open-ended or multiple-choice questions, the latter typically giving more consistent results)
- the clarity of marking criteria
- the number of tasks in the assessment
- the conditions under which the assessment is conducted (such as the time of day or the noise levels)
- the moderator (as teachers can mark questions, particularly open-ended ones, subjectively). This can be termed the level of inter-rater reliability – imagine two teachers marking the same essay and getting similar results).

Now, let's think about validity: the question of whether an assessment measures what we actually want it to measure. Poor validity would be like using a ruler to measure temperature, rather than a thermometer! The main things to consider include the following.

- **Content validity**: Does the assessment cover everything we've taught?
- **Construct validity**: Are we really testing what we think we're testing? For example, are we accidentally just testing pupils' reading ability rather than their understanding of science concepts?
- **Face validity**: Does the assessment make sense to pupils? Would they look at it and think, 'Yes, this is clearly testing what we learned'?

Here's the tricky part: sometimes, making an assessment more reliable means making it less valid, or making it too time-consuming to be practical. For example:

- We could make a test more reliable by adding lots more questions, but then it might take too long to complete and mark.
- Multiple-choice questions are quick to mark and give consistent results, but they don't show us how well pupils can explain their thinking.
- Essay questions might give us better insight into pupil understanding, but they take longer to mark and different teachers might give different grades.

The key is finding the right balance for your purpose. If you're giving a quick quiz to check understanding during a lesson, for example, it doesn't need to be as reliable as an end-of-year exam. For important assessments that affect pupil grades or progression, in contrast, we need to pay extra attention to reliability.

There's no such thing as a perfect assessment: it's about making smart choices based on what you need the assessment to do. It's about finding that sweet spot between getting consistent results, truly measuring what matters, and keeping things practical for both teachers and pupils.

Current statutory guidance

As of the 2015–16 academic year, the UK government introduced a set of interim performance descriptors for primary science, later renamed as Teacher Assessment Frameworks. These frameworks provide teachers with a comprehensive list of 'pupil can' statements to assess each pupil at the end of the relevant key stage.

Key points of the current guidance include the following:

- **Teacher assessment**: National guidance currently recognises that teacher assessment is a valid form of assessment for science at the end of Key Stage 2.
- **Working scientifically**: The ability to 'work scientifically' is a crucial component of the assessment. It can be assessed validly only when pupils are engaged in scientific work such as planning, evaluating and carrying out investigations.
- **Content knowledge**: Scientific vocabulary and factual knowledge can be assessed efficiently through short tests or quizzes administered by teachers at appropriate times.
- **Evidence-based judgement**: To judge that a pupil has met the standard for primary science, teachers need evidence demonstrating consistent attainment of all the statements within the standard, for both 'working scientifically' and for science content.
- **Moderation**: To enhance the reliability of assessments, teachers are encouraged to discuss and compare pupil outcomes and judgements with colleagues, supported by planned criteria and exemplars.
- **Diverse assessment methods**: Teachers are advised to use a range of assessment methods, including observation, questioning, studying products of regular work, and specially designed tasks or tests.
- **Ongoing support**: A programme of ongoing support should be in place to build teachers' capability and confidence in their assessment practices.

Effective assessment in primary science requires a balanced approach that combines formative and summative methods, ensures both reliability and validity, and aligns with curriculum objectives. By following these principles and current guidance, you can create assessment practices that not only measure pupils' attainment accurately but also support and enhance their learning in science.

Some types of pupils' work can be used to make teacher judgements more effectively than others. Examples of these can be found in the 'Teacher assessment exemplification' released by the STA. PLAN has also published a comprehensive set of examples for assessment. You can find links to these resources in the 'Explore further' section at the end of this chapter.

Formative assessment strategies

Evidence shows that formative assessment can lead to substantial improvement in pupil outcomes (Black & William, 1998). The very best teachers collect data on their pupils constantly, and use it to drive learning.

Formative assessment can happen on different timescales. For example, a medium-term timescale might be within and between teaching units. A shorter timescale might be within and between lessons (minute by minute and day by day). The shorter the timescale is, the larger the potential impact on pupils' learning will be. Short-timescale formative assessment is particularly important for checking that misconceptions have been corrected, and for enabling teachers to be responsive in their teaching. It is too late to wait until the end of a unit to do this.

There are a number of formative assessment strategies that can be used to elicit evidence of learning within a lesson. These include:

- listening to pupils during partner work
- using multiple-choice questions that include distractor answers related to misconceptions
- asking pupils to record answers on mini whiteboards
- implementing all-pupil response systems.

All-pupil response systems, although the term is clunky to say, are actually very simple. They are simply mean where the teacher asks a question in such a way that allows them to get a response from every pupil at the same time. For example, pupils showing thumbs-up and thumbs-down could represent positive and negative answers, and holding up fingers 1–5 could represent multiple-choice answers. Regularly getting information from the whole class in this way is a reliable way to assess how a lesson is going.

The strategies that you suggest teachers use will depend on the types of information you want to gather, as well as the types of question they ask. A teacher might want to check, for example, which pupils have remembered whether different materials are conductors or insulators. They might use an all-pupils response system, holding up materials and asking pupils to show a thumbs-up for conductors or thumbs-down for insulators. This would be an efficient way of gathering the data they sought. In contrast, to check whether each pupil is able to explain how a cactus is adapted to a desert environment, the teacher might need them to draw diagrams on their mini whiteboards.

The importance of prior knowledge

Why assess prior knowledge?

The current statutory guidance focuses on two strands of assessment: summatively assessing pupils at the end of key stage, and using formative data collected in lessons to support the resulting judgements. However, it is also important to consider how we assess pupil knowledge *before* we start teaching a unit. Gathering knowledge about pupils' starting points in understanding is important. It means that planning can be adjusted to support learning more effectively. If this 'pre-diagnostic' assessment reveals that lots of pupils are lacking key foundational knowledge, planning can be adjusted to ensure the knowledge is secure before they move on to new learning.

There is a strong evidence base for the premise that learning is more secure when pupils' prior knowledge is taken into account (Howard-Jones et al., 2018). Pupils need to activate their existing knowledge and establish connections between new information and what they already know: this increases the chance of them remembering and applying the concepts we teach. For example, when pupils already know that electricity cannot flow around a broken circuit, they will more quickly and securely grasp how a switch functions.

As we explored further in the section on cognitive science in Chapter 2, pupils acquire new ideas by connecting them to prior knowledge, organising this information into progressively complex schema. It's crucial to sequence teaching carefully to support this process.

Strategies for assessing prior knowledge

You can suggest that teachers use various techniques to gauge current knowledge and understanding at the beginning of a topic. These can be applied with a whole class, small groups or individuals. The 'recognise, reveal and respond' process described below (adapted from EEF guidance Sharples et al., 2024) offers practical strategies.

STAGE	EXPLANATION AND STRATEGIES
Recognise what you want to assess	- In this stage, you decide what knowledge or lack of knowledge you are trying to gauge. - Having a good understanding of the learning journey is important here. You need to know what relevant knowledge has come prior in the curriculum so you can check pupils have retained this before moving on. - Reading around the common preconceptions and misconceptions for any upcoming science topic, and discussing these with colleagues, can help you plan your diagnostic assessment.
Reveal pupils' understanding	There are several assessment activities you can use to reveal pupils' understanding, including: - mind map (with/without physical/pictorial/video prompts) of knowledge related to the topic of focus - big question answers—pupils answer conceptually challenging questions such as, 'What are the properties of a liquid?' - odd one out—pupils discuss 3–4 pictures or objects, explaining which is the odd one out and why - explain a prediction - given the answer—what is the question? - talk for just a minute on … - true/false statements.
Respond in your planning	Lastly, you need to act on the information you have gathered in your planning. For example, you could consider these questions: - Is key vocabulary creating a barrier for understanding? How are you going to address this? - Are there links with previous learning you want to make explicit? How will you do this? - Is there prior learning you need to revisit? - Could the same diagnostic assessment be repeated during or after the topic, to show changes in learning?

Preconceptions and misconceptions

It's not enough just to know what our pupils do and don't understand. We also need to know if there are any areas in which their knowledge is inaccurate.

Pupils start to form ideas about how the world works before their formal science education begins. Different children will have different initial ideas, based on their experiences of the world. These initial ideas are called preconceptions, and they are built through sensory experiences, interactions with objects and living things, and social interactions. Sometimes they align with scientific understanding, but often they do not. If not, they are misconceptions. For example, children might develop the misconception that rain falls from holes in the clouds. This may arise from their early experiences in their own households, where water comes out of holes in the shower head, the tap or a watering can. It's important that we are aware of misconceptions like this, so we can help pupils to form new and scientifically accurate conceptions.

The first step towards supporting pupils to form accurate conceptions is to understand what misconceptions they hold. Lists of common misconceptions to check have been created by subject associations, and these can be good starting points. I also recommend speaking to experienced colleagues and utilising subject networks. These may not be misconceptions held by pupils in your own school, however, so it is important for teachers to gather pupils' ideas at the start of a topic. All of the methods outlined in the section above for gauging prior knowledge can also be used to identify misconceptions.

A few words of caution: be wary of introducing a topic by explaining misconceptions, as you risk pupils remembering only those misconceptions instead of the correct science. Teachers should gather data about what misconceptions pupils hold, but then introduce the topic with the correct science. Teachers can challenge misconceptions with their teaching throughout the topic.

Case study: addressing misconceptions

Alik is a science subject lead in a two-form-entry school in Lincoln. They are new to the school and the role, and their school they have a teaching staff mostly made up of early-career teachers, none of whom have done science past GCSE.

During the first half term, Alik conducts several lesson drop-ins, planning-looks and book-looks to get a sense of the state of science teaching. They find several issues that concern them.

- In one of their Year 5 lesson drop-ins, a pupil puts up her hand to ask whether a plant is a living thing. The teacher says yes but does not elaborate.

- In a reception classroom Alik hears a teacher saying to a pupil, 'Look: all of these objects have sunk to the bottom because they are heavy.'
- In a Year 3 book, they find some pictures of fossils that have been labelled as bones.

It is clear to Alik that both the pupils and the staff hold a number of misconceptions about science. They decide that improving teachers' subject knowledge is going to be their first priority as subject lead.

Alik holds six subject-knowledge PD sessions throughout the year. Three are purely on subject knowledge for the teachers, one each on main topics in biology, chemistry and physics. Each of these is followed by a session on how to address common misconceptions with pupils.

At the end of the year, Alik asks all teachers to complete audits of their confidence in each subject area. Alik uses these to make a plan for continued PD the following year.

Diagnostic questions

One way to identify misconceptions is to use diagnostic questions. These are often multiple-choice questions with options (other than the correct answer) that are designed to demonstrate misconceptions. These are often called plausible distractors. For example, for the beginning of a unit on plants, you might set the following question.
Where do plants get their food?

A) They suck up their food through their roots.

B) *Plants don't need food; they only need water.*

C) *They make their own food in their leaves using sunlight.*

C is the correct answer, but A and B are common misconceptions; that means they can be used to gather information about who holds these misconceptions.

In practice: diagnosing misconceptions with multiple-choice questions

The following multiple-choice questions are examples of ways to diagnose common misconceptions.

TOPIC	DIAGNOSTIC QUESTION	ANSWER	COMMON MISCONCEPTIONS
KS1: Plants	Which of these is not a plant? A) Dandelion B) Fir tree C) Pebble	C	Some pupils may believe that trees are not plants.
KS1: Animals	Which of these are animals? A) Dog B) Grasshopper C) Human D) Apple tree	A, B and C	Some pupils may believe that: • insects are not animals • humans are not animals.
KS1: Living Things	Which of these are living things? A) Rabbit B) Fire C) Tulip D) Fish	A, C and D	Some pupils may believe that: • fire is a living thing • plants are not living things.
Lower KS2: Light	Which of these are light sources? A) Moon B) Sun C) Torch D) Window	B and C	Some pupils may believe that: • the Moon emits light (instead of reflecting it from the Sun) • windows emit light (because light 'comes from the window').
Lower KS2: Magnets	Which of these is magnetic? A) Tin foil B) Plastic cup C) Steel paperclip D) Paper plane	C	Some pupils may believe that all metals are magnetic.

TOPIC	DIAGNOSTIC QUESTION	ANSWER	COMMON MISCONCEPTIONS
Upper KS2: Properties of Materials	Alex puts his soup in an insulating bowl. It stays warm after an hour. Which is the best explanation? A) The insulation keeps the cold from flowing into the soup. B) The insulation stops the heat from flowing out to the air. C) The insulation warms up the soup.	B	Some pupils may believe that: • thermal insulators keep cold in or out • thermal insulators can warm things up.
Upper KS2: Forces	Which of these are planets? A) The sun B) Earth C) The Moon D) Jupiter E) Saturn	B, D and E	Some pupils may believe that: • the Sun is a planet • the Moon is a planet.

Challenging misconceptions

Once we've identified misconceptions, we need to challenge them. Pupils need to be presented with compelling evidence that helps them to change their thinking. This change can take time, and pupils may need to revisit ideas or be shown multiple examples to adjust their thinking. Without concrete proof, it can be hard to change ingrained misconceptions.

Consider the common misconception that heavier objects fall more quickly than lighter objects. This feels like common sense to some people: it is not until we learn about gravity and air resistance that we start to understand why this is not the case. Watching a demonstration (or a video of a demonstration) can be valuable here, and in many other cases too. Sometimes, seeing really is believing!

Changing pupil's ideas can be achieved by providing new information that directly contradicts their beliefs, and then allowing them to revisit and reconstruct their ideas to accept the new theory. This process of contradiction is sometimes referred to as cognitive conflict, and is a useful strategy to promote reorganisation of ideas.

The table below contains further ideas for challenging some key misconceptions. I have put key stages as a rough guide, but remember: pupils of any age can hold a misconception if it hasn't been challenged in their previous educational experiences and so you may well find yourself with a year 6 pupil who still thinks that a plant is not a living thing if this hasn't been successfully challenged further down the school. .

MISCONCEPTION	CHALLENGE
EYFS	
Floating and sinking are dependent on mass.	• Set up a learning area in which pupils can test which objects float and sink, sorting them into two groups. Purposefully provide objects that will challenge misconceptions around mass: for example, choose heavy materials that don't sink (such as wood). • After the activity, have a class discussion. Draw pupils' attention to the fact that not all heavy objects sink. • Set an extra challenge for pupils to find other heavy objects that won't sink.
KS1	
When a solid like sugar dissolves, it has disappeared.	This is a demonstration I like to perform for my pupils: • I stir some salt into a transparent cup of water and let the pupils watch it dissolve. I ask them to put up their hands if they think the salt has disappeared. • I pretend to take a big gulp of water, and dramatically spit it into the sink, saying, 'It hasn't disappeared! I can still taste the salt!' This normally gets some giggles, and proves that the salt is still there. You could also try these demonstrations: • Observe colourful sweets dissolving: the solute spreading out amongst the solvent can be seen clearly. • Dissolve 5g of salt in 100ml of water. Ask pupils to measure the mass of the solution before and after: it will remain constant.

MISCONCEPTION	CHALLENGE
Lower KS2	
Sound travels through only air, not solids or liquids.	• Try the Ogden Trust's Phizzi Practical: Make a hydrophone. This provides an interesting way for to observe that sounds also travel through liquids. • The Marvin and Milo cards from the Institute of Physics suggest other comparative tests to investigate sounds travelling through a variety of materials.
Upper KS2	
Natural selection is an active process: an individual or a species can try to adapt.	Try Phet's online simulator for natural selection. You can play out different scenarios, such as starting with a population of rabbits that have both white and brown fur, and then introducing wolves to see which are most likely to survive. Simulations like this help pupils to see that numbers of rabbits with brown fur increase only through reproduction, and decrease with predation – and that rabbits can't choose to change their fur. It also highlights the element of chance: in each generation, not all rabbits with the desirable trait will survive and not all rabbits with the less-desirable trait will die.

Chapter summary

- Effective assessment combines formative and summative approaches using varied methods, ongoing teacher support and moderation.
- Reliability and validity are crucial, with teachers balancing these based on the purposes of their assessments.
- Assessing pupils' existing knowledge before starting a lesson or unit helps in planning effectively, and ensures that foundational knowledge is secure for new learning.
- Formative assessment is a crucial tool for ensuring pupil progress. Evidence of learning should be elicited through strategies like mini-whiteboard reporting and all-pupil response systems, and then used to adjust teaching.
- It is important to be aware of pupils' preconceptions and misconceptions, and to make plans to address these.

Questions for reflection

- How confident are our teachers in assessing pupils' ability to 'work scientifically'?
- How do our current assessment practices balance the needs for reliability and validity?
- Reflect on the variety of assessment methods you use. Are there any aspects of scientific knowledge or skills that our current methods might be overlooking? Are there other methods we could introduce?
- How do we ensure that our assessments are manageable for both us and our pupils, while still providing meaningful data?
- Is there currently a bank of common misconceptions for the science units taught in our school?
- Do our staff still hold any misconceptions about science?
- Is there space in each lesson and each unit to reflect on data that is collected?

Example PD session: setting multiple-choice questions

Here is an example of what a PD session on setting multiple-choice questions could look like.

TIMING SUGGESTION	SESSION GUIDANCE
10 mins	Share the blog from Joe Kirby on planning multiple-choice questions (cited in the 'Explore further' section below).
5 mins	Discuss how and why this information might be relevant to science teaching, and specifically the topics and pupils that colleagues teach.
15 mins	<ul><li>As a group, brainstorm different approaches to setting multiple-choice questions for pupils: for example, using mini-whiteboards, as 'exit tickets', using pictures or as hinge questions.</li><li>Ask teachers to choose which approaches are most appropriate for them and their classes.</li></ul>

TIMING SUGGESTION	SESSION GUIDANCE
20 mins	• Give teachers the opportunity to draft some multiple-choice questions for an upcoming science topic, and to plan or script how they will introduce these to the pupils. • Ask teachers to rehearse together, providing opportunity for peer feedback.

Explore further

- Rebecca Allen's *What if we cannot measure pupil progress?*: https://rebeccaallen.co.uk/2018/05/23/what-if-we-cannot-measure-pupil-progress/
- *Science Inside the Black Box: Assessment for Learning in the Science Classroom* (2003) by Paul Black and Chris Harrison
- Daisy Christodoulou's *Why is teacher assessment biased?*: https://daisychristodoulou.com/2015/11/why-is-teacher-assessment-biased/
- The EEF's *Improving Primary Science Guidance Report* by Katie Luxton and Bob Pritchard: https://d2tic4wvo1iusb.cloudfront.net/production/eef-guidance-reports/primary-science-ks1-ks2/improving-primary-science-guidance-report-ks1-ks2.pdf?v=1711720513 (see Recommendation 5)
- Joe Kirby's blog How to design multiple-choice questions: https://joe-kirby.com/2014/04/12/mcqdesign/
- *How learning happens: Seminal Works in Educational Psychology and What They Mean in Practice* (2020) by Paul A. Kirschner and Carl Hendrick
- PLAN's Knowledge Matrices resources: https://www.planassessment.com/knowledge-matrices-teacher
- The Primary Science Teaching Trust's Common Misconceptions: https://pstt.org.uk/resources/common-misconceptions/
- *Embedded formative assessment* (2017) by Dylan William

7 Explanations and modelling

> As science teachers and leaders, once we have established what we want our pupils to learn, we have to think about how our exposition is going to lead to this learning. The same key learning principles apply in science as in other subjects:
>
> - Prior knowledge should be activated.
> - Exposition should be broken down into manageable chunks.
> - We should regularly check for pupils' understanding.
>
> In science, we also have to consider that scientific ideas are abstract by their very nature, so they need to be introduced carefully. As science teachers, we have to bridge the gap between the seen and unseen. For example, we might see an apple drop to the floor, but we can't see the gravitational force responsible. We might see the water boiling, but we can't see what is happening to the water particles during this process.
>
> We need to think carefully about how we explain these abstract concepts to pupils, and how we can use multiple diagrams, analogies, models, animations and simulations to do so. In this chapter, we will look at:
>
> - the concept of dual coding, and how visual prompts can aid learning
> - different types and examples of models
> - how scientists use models to represent different kinds of knowledge
> - things to consider when including models in lessons.

Dual coding

Current understanding in cognitive science is that everyone has two cooperating memory systems: a non-verbal system and a verbal system. Research has shown that, if both systems are used at the same time, there are additive effects on memory (Clark & Paivio, 1991). This theory is called 'dual-coding' theory. If we apply dual coding theory to the classroom, then the implications for teacher exposition are that we should present visual information to pupils alongside our verbal exposition.

This is particularly important in science. Here, concepts are abstract, so pupils' imaginations are less likely to create their own images. Let's compare a chunk of exposition where trees are referenced to one where particles are mentioned, for example. The concept of a tree is much more concrete to pupils. They have all seen multiple trees in their everyday lives, so tree images are likely to pop into pupils' heads when we reference them. This is much less likely for the more abstract concept of particles, particularly if they've never seen particle models.

As subject lead, you are able to support teachers in fostering dual coding. They can promote learning of abstract concepts if you provide them with diagrams, pictures, concrete models or videos to go along with their exposition.

Where possible, build up your visual prompts in layers, instead of revealing everything at once: For example, you can draw a diagram under the visualiser that builds as your explanation does. If you were teaching about a food chain you could draw the different parts of it sequentially while explaining, instead of revealing the whole food chain at once. This method helps pupils to follow your thought process step by step; it avoids pupils focusing on the wrong part of the image or experiencing cognitive overload. It also allows you to be more responsive, in real time, to the difficulties pupils may be encountering.

One of the most important aspects of incorporating dual coding is understanding how models can assist with teaching.

Different types of model

Scientific concepts can be complex and difficult to visualise; much of what we study in science is invisible to the naked eye, making models essential tools in the classroom. Models – such as models of the digestive system or the water cycle – simplify these phenomena and make them more accessible. They help us represent, describe, explain and reason about the physical world. Models can be used by the teacher during or after exposition, but pupils can also create their own models as part of a learning sequence.

There are various types of models available. To introduce the role of the heart, for example, we could:

- use a plastic heart (a physical model)
- draw a diagram (a visual model)

- display a heart-monitor reading (a mathematical model)
- clench a fist near our chest (a gestural model)
- explain the heart as two pumps (a verbal model).

The table below details some of the most-useful scientific models for primary science.

TYPE OF MODEL	EXPLANATION/	EXAMPLE
Physical models	A physical model is a 3D object: something concrete that's used to represent a concept.	You might shake sugar cubes and pennies in a jar to represent erosion along a river bed: the sugar cubes would represent soft rock and the pennies harder rock, and the shaking would simulate the movement of the river.
Scale models	Scale models help pupils visualise an idea, process or system that is too small or too large to see.	A scale model of the solar system shows the relative distances between planets.
Analogies	Analogies are verbal models that make links between abstract ideas and relatable real-world situations, linking new and prior knowledge.	Descriptions of water flow could be likened to descriptions of electric current.
Visual models	Visual models include pictures and diagrams, which could be drawn or computer generated.	Drawing circles could represent different particle arrangements in solids, liquids and gases.
Simulations	Simulations are computer models, which are often interactive.	A virtual compass can be moved around an image of a bar magnet to explore its magnetic field. (PhET offers a wide range of other example simulations.)
Historical models	Historical models help to show how ideas change through time. Models increase in sophistication, so often mirror pupils' changing ideas.	The geocentric model of the universe shows how scientists used to believe that the Earth was at the centre of the Universe.

Teaching with models should come after explicit vocabulary teaching, so that pupils are already familiar with the key vocabulary associated with the concept being modelled. It is important to check pupils' understanding, for example by asking questions during and after modelling. For example, ask: 'What part does this part of the model represent?' 'What will happen if…?'

How scientists use models

Models are crucial not only for teaching science but also for advancing scientific understanding. Understanding how and why scientists use models is disciplinary knowledge of which our pupils should be aware.

Scientists continuously refine and create new models to explain the world. As new models are developed and accepted, many older models become outdated but remain useful in classrooms. These historical models help to teach scientific concepts and illustrate the progression of scientific thought. For example, in Key Stage 2, it is common to teach pupils about both the geocentric and the heliocentric models of the universe. This shows pupils how scientists change models as their understanding develops and new evidence comes to light.

Both scientists and pupils reason through models, allowing them to predict, explain and communicate about specific aspects of the world. For example, climate-change models are computer simulations that can demonstrate the shifts for pupils, and also allow scientists to make predictions about the future of Earth's climate system.

Levels of scientific knowledge

In 1991, science professor Alex Johnstone explored the concept of levels of scientific knowledge, exemplifying why models can be so useful. He suggested that there are three levels of knowledge:

- macroscopic: knowledge about easily observable physical phenomena, such as knowledge gained from practical investigations and observations
- symbolic: knowledge about concepts that can be 'seen' only as word or symbol equations that represent them, such as mathematical knowledge represented by formulas, graphs and diagrams
- submicroscopic: knowledge about phenomena that are physical but too small to be seen, such as knowledge of atoms and ions.

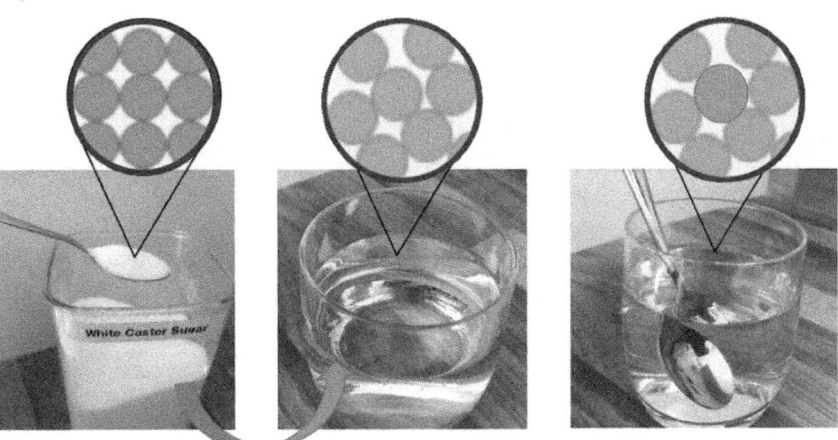

Figure 7.1: Sugar dissolved into water

Pupils need to grasp all three levels to develop a comprehensive understanding of a topic. Experienced scientists can easily transition between these levels, linking macroscopic results with submicroscopic processes and represent their ideas symbolically. Pupils, however, often struggle to connect their understanding at different levels, and models assist pupils in bridging these gaps.

As a science leader, you'll need to ensure that teachers provide models and examples at all levels of knowledge, and that they teach pupils how these are related. The example in Figure 7.1 is an effective model because it shows what happens when a substance dissolves both at the macroscopic (pictures of the sugar and salt) and sub-microscopic level (particle diagrams). The symbolic level could also be shown through a simple word equation: sugar + water → sugary water.

Another example is when teaching electrical circuits, you might instruct pupils to use equipment to make a circuit (as a macroscopic demonstration), show them a computer model of how electrons flow (modelling submicroscopic processes) and draw a circuit diagram (as a symbolic representation).

Limitations and evaluation of models

Although they are powerful tools, we must ensure that models don't confuse pupils or cause misconceptions. We need to choose our models carefully, because each one has limitations.

For instance, consider a physical model of the lungs that's constructed of balloons inside a glass bell-jar. It can demonstrate lung inflation, but it falls short because the chest wall isn't rigid like the glass. The model doesn't show the roles of the ribs and intercostal muscles. Similarly, heart models often depict oxygenated blood as red and deoxygenated blood as blue. This is a misconception I held into my adulthood because of this modelling (and I did a biology degree – oops!).

Pupils might assume models are perfect unless told otherwise, so it's beneficial to provide them with a variety of models for a more comprehensive understanding. To prevent pupils from focusing solely on the model instead of the concept, explicitly highlight the similarities and differences between them.

You could ask the questions below when deciding whether to use a model by evaluating its effectiveness (adapted from EEF, Sharples et al., 2024).

- Does the model accurately represent the scientific concept being taught?
- Does the model show relative sizes or distances accurately? If not, how else can I convey these scales?
- What are the limitations of the model?
- Does the model offer clear, visually appealing, relatable representations of the concept, making it accessible for pupils?
- Does the model make an abstract, complex idea easier to understand and visualise? Are the labels clear? Is the information provided pitched at the right level?
- Does the model accommodate interactivity and engagement?
- Can pupils change features and parameters to explore what happens?

Case study: evaluating how models are used

Anthony is a primary science lead at a one-form-entry school in Plymouth. To deepen his understanding of approaches to the subject, he decides to attend an external science course for subject leaders.

One of Anthony's key takeaways from the sessions was how effective models can aid pupil learning. When he returns to school, he decides that he wants to evaluate how effectively his teachers are currently using models in their science lessons.

Anthony decides to do some lesson drop-ins. However, he first wants to come up with a set of success criteria for effective modelling, so he can make more useful judgements on the modelling he sees.

His success criteria are that:

- key vocabulary is taught before the model is introduced
- the model is appropriate for the concept and aids understanding
- the teacher asks questions throughout to check for understanding
- pupils are made aware of the limitations of the model.

Anthony conducts his drop-ins over the course of the next few weeks. He finds that all but one of his teachers use very limited models in their lessons. Most lessons include just diagrams on slides that accompany the teacher's verbal explanations.

He speaks to the teachers to give them feedback on their lessons, and asks further questions about planning. From these conversations, it appears that teachers don't have a good bank of models to use.

Anthony shares the resources from the science course he attended, which suggested lots of examples of high-quality models. He also shares the success criteria he created.

He conducts further lesson observations three weeks later. He is pleased to see a wider range of modelling in lessons, and most teachers meeting all of the success criteria.

Chapter summary

- Applying dual coding theory, which involves using both verbal and visual information simultaneously, enhances memory and understanding.
- Effective science teaching involves bridging the gap between observable phenomena and abstract scientific concepts. Models are a way of achieving this.
- A model could be a physical 3D representation, scale model, analogy, visual model, computer simulation or historical model.
- Scientists at all levels of expertise, including pupils, can make and use models.

- Teachers can use models during and after explanations, and should continually check pupils' understanding.
- Alex Johnstone's framework describes three levels of scientific knowledge: macroscopic (observable), symbolic (representational) and submicroscopic (atomic). Effective science teaching involves helping pupils connect these levels.
- While models are useful, they have limitations and can sometimes lead to misconceptions. It's crucial to point out the differences between models and the concepts they represent, and to use a variety of models to provide a comprehensive understanding.

Questions for reflection

- To what extent do I and teachers in our school use models in lessons to support understanding?
- Which types of model do we use most frequently: physical, scale, analogy, visual, simulation and/or historical? Why is that?
- Can I think of a recent lesson in which a model significantly helped pupils understand a complex concept? What made it effective?
- Can I identify ways to increase pupil interaction and engagement with models?
- Are our pupils able to identify the limitations of the scientific models in the curriculum?

Example PD session: using models constructively

Here is an example of what a PD session on how best to use models could look like.

TIMING SUGGESTION	SESSION GUIDANCE
15 mins	Share examples of the different types of models in science, and discuss how they enhance learning.
10 mins	Ask teachers to script expositions, including modelling, for their next science lessons. The script should include key questions that they will ask pupils to check for understanding.
10 mins	Ask teachers to practise in pairs, and to give each other feedback.

Explore further

- *Dual Coding With Teachers* (2019) by Oliver Caviglioli
- *Modelling-based Teaching in Science Education* (2016) by John K. Gilbert and Rosária Justi
- 'In defence of the classroom science demonstration' (2021) by Paul McCrory: https://hooktraining.com/defence-of-science-demonstrations/#tab-con-1
- ResearchEDHome 2020's video *Adam Boxer: Dual Coding for Teachers Who Can't Draw: Teacher's Explanations*: https://www.youtube.com/watch?v=16SBht2iF_k
- 'Helping learners think like scientists – why Cambridge Primary and Lower Secondary Science now puts more emphasis on scientific modelling' (2022) by Judith Roberts: https://blog.cambridgeinternational.org/scientific-modelling/
- University of Colorado Boulder's *PhET Interactive Simulations*: https://phet.colorado.edu/

8 Vocabulary

> Language is an important element in every classroom. It is the vehicle through which teachers communicate, break down and impart new learning. In a science classroom, it is how teachers model and explicitly teach the science-specific language that pupils need to understand, build and communicate ideas about science.
>
> As a subject leader, you will need to support your teachers to think carefully about the language they use. Together, you need to consider carefully the way you teach pupils to communicate scientifically, what vocabulary you teach explicitly and how you do this.
>
> In this chapter, we are going to take a look at why teaching vocabulary is so important, how to choose which words to teach, and vocabulary-specific teaching strategies for the science classroom.

Vocabulary: why is it important?

A study by Wexler et al. (2016) found that vocabulary is seldom explicitly taught in science classrooms. This study had a relatively small sample of ten schools, which may be thought not to be representative of the wider picture. However, reports from OFSTED have given support to the claim that vocabulary instruction in primary-school science is not adequate. In commentary on the annual report, Her Majesty's Chief Inspector Amanda Spielman noted: 'Little consideration was given to developing scientific concepts and skills and the vocabulary that comes with being taught science' (2020).

This is a concerning state of affairs, considering research on the importance of vocabulary for children's future academic success. Studies show that the size of a pupil's vocabulary is the best predictor of this, and that pupils with a limited vocabulary at the age of five are four times more likely to struggle with reading as adults (Asmussen et al., 2017).

What makes this even more worrying is that we also know that pupils from disadvantaged backgrounds are more likely to have limited vocabularies. Multiple studies now suggest that area deprivation and socio-economic status negatively impact language skills before pupils enter school (for example,

Roy et al., 2014). This is why high-quality vocabulary instruction in science classrooms is so important. It will not only enable our pupils to be successful academically. It will also ensure that all our pupils, no matter what their start in life is, have the words that they need to comprehend and navigate their science education.

What words should we teach?

The first step in successful vocabulary instruction is deciding which words to teach explicitly. Thousands of words will be uttered by a teacher each lesson, and more encountered in reading and learning resources. There would not be time, nor would it be advisable, to teach all of them. Conscious choices need to be made by you and the teachers as to what words to teach.

Words need to be chosen based on how important they are for pupils' understanding of the topic, and how frequently they will encounter those words in their learning. Once chosen, those words need to be encountered multiple times across a learning sequence. A deep understanding of fewer words is better than understanding lots of words at a surface level (Beck et al., 2013).

It can be helpful to think about three tiers of vocabulary (Beck et al., 2013) when considering word selection. The table below lays out an explanation with examples of each tier of words.

VOCABULARY TIER	EXPLANATION	EXAMPLES
Tier 1	Common, everyday words that are typically learnt through conversation.	book, boy, walk, cat, yellow
Tier 2	Words that are more sophisticated and lesson common than tier 1 words. They are useful across subject areas.	analyse, predict, contribute, excellent, fortunate, measure, obvious, complex, occur
Tier 3	Specialised terms that are typically associated with specific subjects or fields.	photosynthesis, evaporation, voltage, particle, ecosystem, habitat, translucent, respiration

Educators often emphasise the importance of teaching Tier 2 and Tier 3 words, and for good reason. These words contribute significantly to a pupil's ability to understand tricky texts, engage in critical thinking and succeed academically. While Tier 1 words are generally picked up naturally, teaching a wide range of Tier 2 and Tier 3 words can greatly improve a pupil's language skills and academic performance across subjects.

In a science lesson, Tier 3 vocabulary is undoubtedly important for pupils' understanding of given topics. A pupil wouldn't be able to understand fully how a circuit works without understanding the word 'voltage', for example. A good grasp of Tier 3 vocabulary is also needed for pupils to be able to communicate their ideas about science effectively. Any explanation of what happens to water when it is heated that doesn't use the word 'evaporation' would be incomplete. It is important, then, that teachers are able to identify the necessary Tier 3 vocabulary for each unit, and to ensure that it is taught well.

Tier 2 vocabulary also needs to be considered carefully. Research shows that pupils lack understanding of science-relevant Tier 2 words such as 'appropriate', 'determine', 'effect', 'illustrate', 'generate', 'interpret' and 'relative' (Tao, 1994). These are words that could be crucial to understanding. For example, if a pupil does not have a good understanding of the word 'affect', they are going to struggle to answer the question 'What do you think could affect the voltage in this circuit?' It's easy to see how a teacher in a Key Stage 1 classroom might spend lots of time teaching why different materials are appropriate for different objects. If the word 'appropriate' is never explicitly taught and understood, though, use of the term may create a barrier to understanding and communication.

There are some words that will need to be defined or reviewed quickly because they are essential for understanding a part of the content. However, teachers may choose not to spend extended time on them because other words are more important: lesson time is a limited resource. Have a look at the lesson extracts below, which show possible choices a teacher may make about vocabulary in each lesson.

In practice: identifying key vocabulary

The table below shows possible choices a teacher may make about vocabulary in each text extract.

Tier 3: Teach in the moment	Tier 3: Teach explicitly	Tier 2: Teach explicitly
EYFS		
Charlie was building a hut in the garden. He'd built strong walls, and added a <u>waterproof</u> roof and a soft carpet. Now he needed to find the perfect windows. Soon he had a <u>solution</u>: he could use something <u>transparent</u>. He felt like a proper <u>engineer</u> now!		
waterproof transparent	engineer	solution
KS1		
The <u>temperature</u> in the United Kingdom is <u>variable</u>. We can measure the temperature by using a <u>thermometer</u>. If the temperature is hot, the <u>mercury</u> in the thermometer will rise.		
temperature thermometer	mercury	variable
KS2		
Living <u>organisms</u> have <u>adaptations</u> that help them to survive. For example, kangaroo rats have special organs that stop them from getting <u>dehydrated</u>. The animals and plants in one habitat are suited to living there, and may not be able to survive in other habitats. When a habitat changes, the animals and plants that live there are <u>affected</u>.		
organisms adaptations	dehydrated	affected

It is worth noting that the tier to which you may assign a word is dependent on the age and knowledge of your pupils. For example, the words 'organs' and 'habitats' from the example above could be classed as Tier 3 vocabulary in a Key Stage 1 classroom, where pupils have not encountered these words before.

One more type of word to consider is polysemous words. These are words that have everyday meanings as well as specific scientific meanings, such as 'slide', 'attract' and 'pole'. Pupils need to be taught the scientific meanings of these words explicitly to avoid confusion.

Case study: ensuring consistent vocabulary instruction across the school

Monika is a science subject lead at a three-form-entry primary school in Cheshire. On the school development plan this year, vocabulary was named as an area of focus. Her line manager asked her to go to their next meeting with an action plan for science.

Monika wants to go to her meeting with lots of data for reflection, so she does some lesson drop-ins and planning-looks focused on vocabulary. She notices that vocabulary instruction is not consistent: only some teachers, not all, teach key terms explicitly. She also notices that not all teachers are using the same definitions. For example, the definition of 'habitat' given by a Year 2 teacher was different from the one given by a Year 4 teacher.

To address the issue, Monika decides that she first needs to ensure vocabulary definitions are consistent. She creates a vocabulary bank of key words for each science unit, setting out the definitions to use. She then runs a PD session in which she introduces the new vocabulary bank. She also begins to go over strategies for how to teach vocabulary explicitly.

Monika reports her suggestions to her line manager, who agrees with the approach. Monika's manager suggests that she work together with the humanities lead, who has observed similar inconsistencies in his department.

To further their aims, Monika and the humanities lead decide to redesign their end-of-unit assessments to include vocabulary sections. This means they can regularly gather data on pupils' knowledge of key vocabulary across year groups.

Teaching strategies

Once we have chosen the words on which we are going to focus, how should we teach them? Quigley (2018) suggests following the SEEC model:

- select
- explain
- explore
- consolidate.

The previous section of this chapter covered the 'select' part of this model, so let's begin here with 'explain'.

Explain

When explaining new words to pupils, it is advisable to:

- say the word clearly
- write the word
- give a pupil-friendly definition
- give multiple meaningful examples.

When giving multiple meaningful examples in science teaching, it can be beneficial to model the new word in context. For example, if you have taught the definition of the word 'repel', you may then want to demonstrate using a pair of magnets: 'When I put the north poles of the magnets together, they repel. They push away.' Next, you may give the pupils a chance to use the word in a similar context: 'Tell your partner what happens when I put the south poles of the two magnets together.'

Research shows that it is advantageous to pair new words with images, which could be in any form: photographs, drawings or symbols, for example. When pupils are taught new vocabulary alongside images, both their immediate and delayed recall of the words improves (Cohen & Johnson, 2012).

It can also be useful to show pupils how to segment some words according to their morphemes (the smallest units of meaning within words). This can result in new words with similar morphemes being understood more easily (Quigley et al., 2018). For example:

The tables below show common prefixes and suffixes used in science (from Markwick, 2018).

PREFIX	MEANING
an	against
aero	air
acou	sound
anti	against
bio	life
cardi	heart
carn	flesh
centi	hundred
chloro	green
di	two
dent	tooth
endo	in
exo	out
equi	equal
homo	same
herb	plant

PREFIX	MEANING
hetero	different
hydro	water
inter	between
macro	large
micro	small
mono	one
noct	night
phono	sound
photo	light
poly	many
pre	before
re	again / back
sub	under
tele	distant
therm	heat

SUFFIX	MEANING
costal	rib
derm	skin
graph	writing

SUFFIX	MEANING
pod	foot
sope	look at
septic	rotting

SUFFIX	MEANING
meter	measure
morph	shape
ology	study
phyll	leaf

SUFFIX	MEANING
sphere	globe
synthesis	putting together
vore	swallow

Explore

Further exploration of a word is not always necessary or advisable given other constraints and material to learn within the lesson but for the most important words it important to spend time making sure pupils securely understand them and they have been embedded. There are a multitude of options for how to do this but here are some suggestions with examples.

TYPE OF ACTIVITY	EXAMPLE
Actions	When teaching words such as 'solids', 'liquids' and 'gases', the teacher could associate an action with each. For example, for 'solid', pupils could shape both hands into fists and quickly shake them close together to suggest vibrating particles in a solid. The teacher would then call out the words randomly, prompting pupils to show the appropriate action for each word.
Word associations	After having given definitions for the words 'gravity', 'friction' and 'force', the teacher could ask pupils to associate one of their new words with a presented word or phrase. For example: • Which word goes with 'falling'? (gravity) • Which word goes with 'push'? (force) • Which word goes with 'slowing down'? (friction)
Cloze sentences	After having taught the words 'stem', 'flower' and 'leaf', the teacher could ask pupils to put each of the words into the correct sentence. For example: • The _____ is where the plant makes its food. (leaf) • The bee landed on the brightly coloured _____. (flower) • After a day without water, the _____ began to droop. (stem)
Examples and non-examples	After teaching the definition of 'transparent', the teacher could provide a range of materials that are transparent and those that are not, and ask pupils to sort them.

TYPE OF ACTIVITY	EXAMPLE
Definition bingo	After teaching multiple words, the teacher could ask pupils to draw (or could provide) bingo grids with up to nine squares. Pupils would then choose up to nine of the words they have learned, and write each in a box. The teacher would read out the definitions and, if pupils have the word that matches, they'd cross it out. When they get a row full of crosses, they call out 'Bingo!'

Consolidate

We know that, to understand a word deeply, we need to be exposed to that word repeatedly. Multiple studies have found correlations between repeated exposure to words and learning (Uchihara et al., 2019). We also need to allow for a little forgetting before retrieving the word again: the effort strengthens how well we remember it. Therefore, it is important that words are revisited across a learning sequence. Pupils should have multiple chances to encounter them, to retrieve their prior knowledge of their meanings.

Pupils who need additional support

It is likely that some pupils will require additional support with learning vocabulary, perhaps because of SEND or EAL requirements. The best way of supporting these pupils is to increase the number of times they are being exposed to new vocabulary: repetition is key. Decide on a limited number of the most crucial words or phrases for each topic, and preteach these to pupils before the lesson or topic. Preteaching, reteaching and specific vocabulary interventions can all be used to increase the number of times pupils encounter key words.

Adding multisensory aspects to the teaching of new topic vocabulary using objects, pictures, photos and gestures can be helpful, too. Pupils could also be given key word lists or vocabulary mats to scaffold their spoken and written language in lessons.

Chapter summary

- Vocabulary proficiency correlates with academic success and is particularly crucial for pupils from disadvantaged backgrounds.
- Teachers should focus on teaching:
  - tier 2 words: high-frequency, often literary or formal words
  - tier 3 words: low-frequency subject-specific words
  - polysemous words: words with both basic and specialist meanings.
- It is important for vocabulary teaching to be regular and consistent across all year groups.
- The SEEC model (Select, Explain, Explore and Consolidate) can be a helpful guideline for teaching vocabulary.
- Pupils should be exposed to both simple, child-friendly definitions of words and engaging ways to incorporate these into their lexicons.
- Repeated exposure to words and spaced retrieval practice are essential for vocabulary retention and deep understanding.

Questions for reflection

- Are the science teachers in my school clear on what words they should be teaching?
- Are there consistent strategies for teaching vocabulary embedded my school's science classrooms?
- How can we ensure that vocabulary is revisited and embedded over time?
- How can we support pupils who need additional support with vocabulary learning?

Example PD session: teaching vocabulary

Here is an example of what a PD session on teaching vocabulary could look like.

TIMING SUGGESTION	SESSION GUIDANCE
Before the session	Source some example extracts of information texts related to the teachers' current science topics.
5 mins	Discuss the link between academic success and vocabulary knowledge.
10 mins	Use the 'What words should we teach?' section of this chapter to explain the different types of vocabulary to teach explicitly (Tier 3, Tier 2 and polysemous words).
10 mins	Give teachers the example extracts and ask them to work in pairs to identify the types of words in the text.
5 mins	Use the 'Explore' section of this chapter to give some examples of strategies for explicit vocabulary teaching (such as 'Actions' and 'Cloze sentences').
15 mins	Give teachers the opportunity to script a short vocabulary session for their next science lesson and then to rehearse these together, with the opportunity for peer feedback.

Explore further

- The EEF's *Unlocking the language of science: strategies for teaching science vocabulary* (2024) by Rachael Cuthbert: https://educationendowmentfoundation.org.uk/news/eef-blog-unlocking-the-language-of-science-strategies-for-teaching-scientific-vocabulary
- *Vocabulary Ninja* (2024) by Andrew Jennings
- The EEF's *Improving Primary Science Guidance Report* by Katie Luxton and Bob Pritchard: https://d2tic4wvo1iusb.cloudfront.net/production/eef-guidance-reports/primary-science-ks1-ks2/improving-primary-science-guidance-report-ks1-ks2.pdf?v=1711720513 (see Recommendation 1)
- *Bringing Words to Life* (2013) by Isabel L. Beck, Margaret G. McKeown and Linda Kucan
- *Closing the Vocabulary Gap* (2018) by Alex Quigley

9 Practical science

> Practical science is, and should be, a large part of any science curriculum – and of many science lessons. It is part of what makes science 'science' and distinct from other subjects. What exactly do we mean by 'practical science', though? There's not just one accepted definition, but we can think of it as this: a wide variety of activities in which pupils manipulate or observe real objects and materials, to prompt thinking about the world in which we live.
>
> Practical science should be 'hands on' wherever possible, but it could also include teacher demonstrations and modelling of scientific concepts. In this chapter, we are going to look at why teaching practical science is important, the different skills and enquiry types to teach and how to teach these well.

Why teach practical science?

Science is an empirical subject. This means that science relies on observation and experimentation to gather evidence and gain knowledge. Practical work is an inherent part of the field of science, so it also needs to be a crucial component of science teaching. The largest scientific professional bodies (The Royal Society of Biology, Royal Society of Chemistry and Institute of Physics), the Wellcome Trust and the Association for Science Education are all strong supporters of practical science.

There is a wealth of reasons why practical science is important in our curriculums and in our lessons. For example, it:

- fosters engagement and positive scientific attitudes (Ofsted, 2013)
- has a positive impact on progress and attainment (Ofsted, 2011)
- facilitates conceptual understanding, bringing theory to life
- models how scientists think and work
- develops skills needed in further science study and scientific careers
- develops transferable skills such as planning, teamwork and communication.

> ### Case study: supporting practical work
>
> Marie is a subject lead in a four-form-entry school in Portsmouth. During her learning walks over the course of a term, she notices that the majority of lessons are missing practical elements. The practical elements that are included are mostly teacher demonstrations.
>
> Marie speaks to each of her science teachers. The conversations suggest that many of them feel there is not enough time in lessons to complete practical activities, and that some are worried about behaviour. It feels easier just to demonstrate from the front.
>
> Marie decides to run a PD session reminding staff of the importance of practical work. It focuses on how clear expectations, planning and routines around practical work can support with time efficiency and behaviour. She films herself and another teacher who is confident in practical work to show as an example.
>
> After the PD session, Marie identifies some teachers who need further support. She sets up some co-planning time with them to support them with planning successful practical investigations.

Enquiry skills

Terminology

When talking about practical science, it is useful to know that multiple terms can be used interchangeably. 'Enquiry skills', 'inquiry skills', 'investigative work' and 'working scientifically' are all terms that are generally used to mean a range of processes and methods that answer questions in science. The current terminology used by the National Curriculum for England is 'working scientifically'. It defines this as 'understanding of the nature, processes and methods of science through different types of science enquiries that help [pupils] to answer scientific questions about the world around them'.

Although many terms are interchangeable, it is important to make a distinction between 'scientific enquiry' and 'enquiry-based learning'. Scientific enquiry is a curriculum area, whereas enquiry-based learning is a style of lesson.

Enquiry skills, not enquiry-based learning

In enquiry-based learning, pupils are expected to discover the curriculum content of the lesson for themselves, through experimentation. For example, in the first lesson of a unit on electricity, a teacher would give their pupils all the equipment to make a circuit and expect them to find out for themselves how to do that. Pupils would be left to discover for themselves why certain things work or don't work. Advocates of this approach say that this type of lesson can boost pupils' engagement, and that it mirrors how scientists acquire knowledge in the real world.

The problem is that scientists in the real world are experts, with a huge amount of prior knowledge. In contrast, our primary-aged pupils are very much still novices: they need teachers to activate their prior knowledge and manage the cognitive load of the lesson. Research suggests that minimal-guidance enquiry-based learning is less effective than direct instruction. (Kirschner et al., 2006; Jerrim et al., 2022). We should teach scientific enquiry *skills*, as these are important parts of all curriculums. Research shows, however, that we shouldn't teach them, nor any other part of the curriculum, through an enquiry-based approach.

Types of enquiry skill

A broad array of skills and enquiry types fall under the umbrella of enquiry skills. I have found it helpful to think about them in four main categories:

1. Gathering information by observing and using secondary sources
2. Questioning, predicting and planning
3. Interpreting information and drawing conclusions
4. Communicating results and evaluating.

The main enquiry types stated in the National Curriculum for England are:

- observing over time
- pattern-seeking
- identifying, classifying and grouping

- comparative and fair testing
- researching using secondary sources.

The following list is drawn from the InterAcademy Partnership's suggestions for inquiry-based science education (Harlen & Allende, 2006). These include:

- collecting data through direct observation of events or researching from various sources
- exploring questions they've personally identified as interesting, even when introduced by instructors
- developing additional questions that can spark new investigations
- forming predictions based on their current understanding
- engaging in scientific discussions with classmates or teachers about their observations
- communicating ideas using appropriate scientific language and representations
- suggesting experimental methods to test their own or others' hypotheses
- contributing to the planning of investigations that include proper controls
- confidently and correctly using measurement tools and equipment
- working to solve problems independently
- consulting diverse information sources to gather necessary facts
- evaluating the reliability and usefulness of ideas based on evidence
- considering alternative viewpoints beyond their own
- critically examining their research methods and outcomes.

The following table elaborates on enquiry types based on recommendations by the Primary Science Teaching Trust and Ogden Trust. Alongside each type of enquiry, we dive into what each of it means in a bit more detail. As a science leader, you might want to read this list and consider how regularly each of these skills currently features in lessons in your school.

TYPE OF ENQUIRY	EXPLANATION	EXAMPLE ENQUIRY QUESTIONS
Fair and comparative testing	These types of test involve changing only one variable (the independent variable) in order to observe the effect on another variable (the dependent variable).	<ul><li>How does changing the height of the ramp affect the speed of the car?</li><li>Will plants grow taller in the light or in the dark?</li><li>How does adding different amounts of sand to soil affect how quickly water drains through it?</li><li>How does the volume of a drum change as you move further away from it?</li></ul>
Pattern-seeking	These investigations involve making observations, including measurements, and looking for patterns in their data. They are not fair or comparative tests because certain variables can't be controlled.	<ul><li>Does the wind always blow in the same direction?</li><li>Which habitat do worms prefer?</li><li>Does the size and shape of a magnet affect how strong it is?</li><li>Do all flowers have the same number of petals?</li></ul>
Identifying and classifying	In this type of enquiry, observations are used to find similarities and differences. These can indicate connections and ways in which subjects can be grouped.	<ul><li>How can we sort these leaves into groups?</li><li>How do the skeletons of different animals compare?</li><li>Which materials will let electricity go through them, and which will not?</li><li>Can we use the classification keys to identify all the animals that we found when pond-dipping?</li></ul>
Model-based testing	These investigations use models to simulate real-life conditions, and are used to test whether ideas and explanations make sense. They can also be used to explain abstract ideas by providing concrete representations.	<ul><li>How can we model the phases of the moon using torches and relevant-size balls?</li><li>What can using tweezers, pegs and spoons tell us about how different birds' beaks are suited to different seeds?</li><li>Can we use tights to demonstrate how intestines work?</li></ul>

TYPE OF ENQUIRY	EXPLANATION	EXAMPLE ENQUIRY QUESTIONS
Observing over time	These are enquiries related to changes observed over a period of time. This could be of any length, from seconds to many years. They lend themselves to observations of the natural world, but can also be used to compare materials and observe other physical processes.	• How do shadows change throughout the day? • Would a paper boat float forever? • How does a nail in salt water change over time? • How does a bean plant change each week?
Researching using secondary sources	These investigations involve finding the answers to scientific questions by exploring others' work. Sources could include pictures, books, websites, preprepared information sheets, museums or conversations with experts.	• Why is drinking salt water bad for humans? • How are bricks made? • What kinds of plant grow in rainforests? • How have our ideas about the solar system changed over time?

Principles of good practical work

Although there are many reasons to include practical work in our curriculums and our lessons, it is important to remember that those skills are just one part of what makes a great scientist. Pupils also need to learn lots of knowledge and facts and these are best acquired through direct instruction. The National Curriculum for England is very clear that 'working scientifically' skills should not be taught in isolation. Rather, they should be woven into knowledge content where relevant. This means that, while we want to ensure that our curriculums and lessons have lots of practical content, we never want to do a practical that doesn't link directly to our unit or lesson.

For example, in a unit on plants, it would make sense for pupils to complete an 'observation over time' enquiry such as observing a bean plant grow. In a unit on fossils, identifying and classifying might be the main enquiry type. Similarly, some units will involve less practical work than others. It would be natural for a unit on habitats, for example, to include fewer practical enquiries than one on electrical circuits which might be very enquiry based and that is OK and appropriate!

It's also important to remember that full-blown scientific investigations are not always needed. It might be that we just focus in on a few skills or techniques each lesson. In one lesson, for example, we might present pupils with already-collected data for them to analyse. In another lesson, we might ask them to use their observation skills by comparing photographs.

A report by the Science Community Representing Education, 'Getting practical: a framework for practical work in science' (STEM Learning, 2009), states that high-quality practical work should be:

- integrated into all science long-term schemes of learning, so that most lessons will include some hands-on activity to provide a stimulating learning environment
- well planned, through inclusion in medium-term schemes of learning and lesson plans, so that resource provision and class management can be organised effectively
- time-efficient, so that the time-consuming requirements of practical work are balanced against the pressure of covering curriculum content.

As subject leads, then, we don't need to pack every lesson full of practicals: we just need to have done the curriculum thinking that ensures pupils are exposed to a wide range of practical skills and enquiries during their learning journey as a whole.

Safety guidance

Lastly, but not unimportantly, all good practical work must adhere to safety guidance. Good sources of support for science leaders in this area are the health and safety resources from the ASE and the Consortium of Local Education Authorities for the Provision of Science Services (CLEAPSS).

- The ASE's resources, and specifically its book *Be Safe!*, cover all aspects of health and safety in primary-school science. It's a useful starting point for science leaders as it covers key considerations for topics covered in primary science, such as keeping animals in school.
- CLEAPSS provides an online resource that presents advice on ways to carry out practical activities so that they are functional, safe and effective for

supporting learning. Many schools have memberships through their local authorities.

Science leaders should be clear on the relevant health and safety guidance for the practical activities that take place in their school. This guidance can then be disseminated to teachers through training. You could also distil the most-important considerations for each unit, and include them in your medium-term plans.

In practice: a model for guiding pupils to work scientifically

In the *Improving Primary Science Guidance Report* (2024), the EEF lays out a seven-step model (adapted from Quigley et al., 2021) for fostering enquiry skills. Based on that model, a practical science lesson might look like the example below.

STEP	EXPLANATION
1. Activating prior knowledge	Teachers should: • connect new learning to prior knowledge • determine what pupils already know • compare this to what they need to understand, in order for them to access the lesson • guide the lesson's pace and content based on this information.
2. Explicit strategy instruction	Teachers should: • explicitly teach the knowledge, skills and processes required for pupils to work scientifically • define the learning objectives clearly • address common misconceptions early, to prevent them from becoming ingrained.
3. Modelling of learned strategy	Teachers should enhance understanding by: • using demonstrations • modelling expected behaviour or thinking • offering examples, partially completed examples or non-examples.
4. Memorisation of strategy	Teachers should: • check for understanding, for example by using low-stakes quizzes on particular strategies • gather data from as many pupils as possible when making decisions about next steps in learning.

STEP	EXPLANATION
5. Guided practice	Teachers should: • incorporate practical activities to reinforce learning, aid recall, and deepen understanding while developing scientific skills • clearly define the learning outcomes for these activities • determine how to measure achievement.
6. Independent practice	Teachers should: • gradually decrease levels of support as pupils expand their knowledge and expertise • encourage greater independence.
7. Structured reflection	Teachers should: • encourage discussion and reflection • create opportunities for pupils to summarise their learning and receive feedback (for example, by asking questions like, 'Does the conclusion make sense? Why? What improvements could you make?'

The seven steps can be applied over a series of lessons or throughout a topic. While the steps are sequential, in practice there will be some overlap and repetition. For instance, you might need to check pupils' understanding on particularly challenging topics more frequently. Opportunities for discussion and reflection should be woven in throughout.

Behaviour during practical activities

Behaviour is important to consider during practical activities. Practical activities can provide opportunities for poor behaviour, largely due to changes in normal classroom practice: pupils are, for example, asked to work in new groups, move around the classroom and use unfamiliar equipment. Indeed, behaviour can be one of the reasons why teachers may be reluctant to carry out practical activities in their lessons. However, good behaviour in a practical is vital, both for safety reasons and so that pupils actually meet the activity's learning goals.

Remember, most pupils absolutely love doing practical science, so motivation is your best tool. It allows you to set high expectations: you can be clear that, if any pupils do not meet those expectations, they will not be allowed to take part. This clear boundary can work wonders.

Below are some strategies for holding successful practical investigations. You could consider sharing them with teachers during PD sessions, or incorporating them in planning.

- Test and set up experiments and demonstrations in advance of the lesson.
- Make sure all pupils can see demonstrations and modelling.
- Don't hand out equipment until after giving instructions.
- Go through key safety points.
- Set very clear expectations before pupils start. For example: 'If you get out of your seat, or do not stop when I ask you to, you will sit out for the rest of the experiment.'
- Narrate what you want to see and give incentives.
- Have clear routines for handing out and collecting equipment.
- Plan groupings, thinking about who will work well together. Keeping pupils in the same groups for every practical will save time in lessons.
- If your classroom is not set up with grouped tables already, decide how you will set these up for the experiment. For example, you could decide that the front row will turn their chairs around to face the second. Practice this with pupils in your first lesson, and keep the same system every time.
- Assign pupils numbers and roles. For example: 'If you are Person 1, you are filling up the measuring cylinder with water. If you are Person 2, you are timing one minute on the stopwatch.'
- Leave enough time to clear up.

It is very much worth the time at the beginning of each year to set up these routines and expectations. If you spend time practising and embedding these routines early on, you will save lots of time for the rest of the year. They will also mean that behaviour during practicals is conducive to learning.

Pupils who need extra support

Some pupils will need extra support when it comes to practical work. The support required will depend on their barrier to learning. The main barriers to consider here are motor difficulties (which may mean pupils struggle with certain pieces of equipment), difficulties with social skills (which may mean pupils find group work challenging), memory difficulties and language difficulties. Below are some suggestions for support.

TYPE OF DIFFICULTY	SUGGESTIONS FOR WAYS TO ASSIST
Motor difficulties	• adapted equipment, such as larger tweezers, easy-grip scissors and measuring equipment with larger intervals • writing scaffolds, such as ready-drawn tables for pupils to fill in • alternatives to written recording, such as videos • specific group roles that suit pupils' abilities
Social communication difficulties	• groups that include supportive peers with whom pupils work well • time taken before practicals to explain some details using social stories • smaller groups • assigned roles • sentence stems
Memory difficulties	• written copies of the method • visual aids, such as images of the different steps in the method • worked examples or demonstrations left out for all to see • instructions broken down into manageable chunks
Language difficulties	• sentence stems • word banks • visual aids, such as images of equipment

Demonstrations

Demonstrations also fall into the category of practical science, and can be very valuable parts of science lessons. Sometimes, they aren't sufficient alone. For example, if the aim of the practical activity is for pupils to learn how to use a piece of scientific equipment, a demonstration would not be enough: pupils would need to handle the equipment themselves afterwards. However, if the aim is to develop pupils' knowledge and understanding of the natural world, for example, teachers have a choice: pupils could take part in a 'hands on' practical activity or watch a teacher-led demonstration.

You might choose a demonstration over a practical activity when:

- experiments are too risky or complicated for pupils to perform independently
- financial limitations prevent having enough equipment for all pupils
- time constraints require a quicker alternative to group work
- you need to focus pupil attention on specific teaching points through targeted questioning
- you want pupils to focus on understanding concepts rather than managing equipment
- you need to model the correct use of equipment before a different lesson's group practical activity, or to reinforce key teaching points following one.

To run a good demonstration, teachers should have:

- prepared equipment in advance
- thought about how all pupils will be able to see the demonstration (for example, using a visualiser)
- planned key questions and key learning points to emphasise.

Chapter summary

- Practical science involves hands-on activities, teacher demonstrations and modelling, all of which can help pupils understand scientific concepts by manipulating or observing what is around them.
- Practical science fosters engagement, enhances progress and attainment, facilitates conceptual understanding, models scientific thinking and develops important skills.
- Skills developed through practical science include observing, questioning, predicting, planning, using equipment, solving problems, assessing evidence and reflecting critically.
- Enquiry types include fair testing, pattern-seeking, identifying and classifying, modelling, observing over time, and researching secondary sources.
- Practical activities should be integrated when they are suited to the knowledge content being taught.

- Attention to safety guidance and good behaviour is vital.
- The seven-step model for teaching scientific enquiry includes activating prior knowledge, explicit instruction, modelling, memorisation, guided practice, independent practice and structured reflection.
- Support should be tailored to pupils' specific difficulties.

Questions for reflection

- Do teachers understand the merits of running practical lessons?
- Does my curriculum include a clear progression of practical skills?
- Does my curriculum include a balance of different enquiry types?
- What would my pupils say if I ask them how a scientist answers questions?

Example PD session: planning for practical work

Here is an example of what a PD session on how to incorporate practical work in lessons could look like.

TIMING SUGGESTION	SESSION GUIDANCE
Before the session	Ask teachers to bring their medium-term plans for science lessons.
10 mins	Use this chapter (especially the sections on types of enquiry skill and principles of good practical work) to provide guidance on practical work in science.
10 mins	• Ask teachers to look at their upcoming units of work, and to identify which concepts would benefit from practical work. • Ask them to map out which lessons will contain practical work.
10 mins	Model how to plan a practical investigation, considering: • key learning objectives and questions for discussion • modelling skills • planning behaviour routines, roles and groups • considering pupils who will need extra support.

TIMING SUGGESTION	SESSION GUIDANCE
15 mins	• Direct teachers to choose one upcoming practical lesson, and to plan its investigation. • Ask teachers to share their plans with partners, and to exchange feedback.

Explore further

- The EEF's *Improving Primary Science Guidance Report* (2024) by Katie Luxton and Bob Pritchard: https://d2tic4wvo1iusb.cloudfront.net/production/eef-guidance-reports/primary-science-ks1-ks2/improving-primary-science-guidance-report-ks1-ks2.pdf?v=1711720513 (see Recommendation 3)
- The Ogden Trust's 'Working scientifically' resources: https://www.ogdentrust.com/resources/?curriculum=&age=&series=working-scientifically
- The Primary Science Teaching Trust's *Types of Enquiry*: https://pstt.org.uk/resources/enquiry-approaches/
- Science Sparks's *Science Experiments for Kids* resources: https://www.science-sparks.com/
- *Working Scientifically: A Guide For Primary School Teachers* (2016) by Kevin Smith

10 Dialogue

> Dialogue is an important part of the learning process, so it's a vital thing to consider in the classroom.
>
> Dialogue might be between two or more pupils, during a group task or practical experiment. It might be between the teacher and a specific pupil. It might involve the whole class, when the teacher bounces and extends talk between different pupils with prompts and questions.
>
> The skills involved in using spoken language to communicate effectively are termed 'oracy'. We want our pupils to develop great oracy, to be able to communicate their ideas about science and the world successfully. Good oracy doesn't come about without teachers modelling great talk and facilitating learning through dialogue in their classrooms.
>
> In this chapter, we are going to look at:
>
> - routines and stimuli to support oracy and encourage dialogue
> - different types of talk that are important in science lessons
> - stimuli for encouraging scientific discussions.

Advantages of dialogue

Dialogue is pupils' primary vehicle for communicating their ideas about science. There are lots of reasons why promoting talk is important for them: it allows them to develop their own ideas by 'thinking aloud', it can be used to extend thinking and deepen learning, and it gives pupils a chance to rehearse their ideas orally before sharing them more widely or writing them down.

For teachers, lots can be gleaned from pupils' talk. It can be a great means for formative assessment, and can draw out misconceptions. Talk in a classroom also supports engagement: many pupils love to share, discuss and debate their ideas with their classmates. It also enables pupils who struggle with written communication to show their science understanding.

Routines that encourage dialogue and support oracy

Dialogue is conversation that happens in the classroom, and oracy is the skillset needed to accomplish it effectively: the ability to articulate ideas and express them fluently. As a science lead, you'll need to promote rich dialogue during lessons, helping teachers to support pupils' oracy skills and scientific vocabulary.

A number of routines can be put in place in order to enable this, some of which are included in the table below.

ROUTINE	EXPLANATION AND EXAMPLE
Providing guidelines for teachers	Teachers play an important role in supporting, guiding and stretching discussions. The list below includes guidelines for doing this effectively (adapted from Qualter & Harlen, 2014). • Join in without dominating the discussion. • Listen to pupils' answers and encourage them to elaborate (for example, prompting, 'I see', 'Yes', 'Keep going' or 'Say more'). • Ask pupils to explain their thinking. • Probe to clarify meaning. • Avoid giving an impression that only the right answer is acceptable.
Setting ground rules for pupils	It is important to teach pupils explicitly what makes a good discussion, and to set ground rules. These may include the following (adapted from Loxley et al., 2017). • Listen to the speaker. • Include everyone in the discussion. • Ask questions. • Challenge one another's ideas and opinions with respect. • Ask for others' ideas, and give reasons for your own.

Holding pupils accountable	You can build a culture of accountability by asking pupils to repeat back what their classmates have said. If they cannot, hold them to account. An example exchange might be as follows.
	  Teacher: What do you think the similarities between these materials might be, Andy?
	  Andy: I think the similarities are that they are both transparent and flexible.
	  Teacher: Jess, What did Andy say?
	  Jess: I can't remember.
	  Teacher: You need to be listening. That's a demerit. Andy, please would you repeat what you said?

ROUTINE	EXPLANATION AND EXAMPLE
	Andy: They are both transparent and flexible. Teacher: Jess, try again. What did Andy say? Jess: He said they are both transparent and flexible. Teacher: Great – and do you agree? Note how this teacher goes back to the pupil so there is no chance for them to opt out. The teacher also asks Andy to repeat his original point, instead of just repeating it for him. This shows that pupil talk is just as valued as teacher talk, and reinforces that pupils need to listen to everyone, not just the teacher.
Sentence stems for discussion	Sentence stems can be a useful scaffold for discussion. These could be displayed on the board, or permanently in the classroom. For example: • I agree with … because … • I disagree with … because … • I'd like to add … • Another example is … • Couldn't another reason be …? • I used to think … but now I think … • On the one hand … but on the other hand … You could focus on just a few of these sentence stems for younger pupils, and build up the bank as year groups progress.
Talk partners	Assigning pupils 'talk partners' (partners with whom they can talk at specific points in the lesson) is a good strategy for a number of reasons. 1. It boosts participation ratio: everyone is discussing in their pairs. 2. It allows pupils a chance for low-stakes rehearsal of their ideas before sharing them in front of the whole class. 3. You can set mixed-attainment pairs so that higher-attaining pupils can support lower-attaining pupils with their answers. 4. The teacher can circulate and start to get a sense of whose answers might be good to share in the whole-class discussion.

These routines can be used across key stages, and consistency is key. If they can be embedded in EYFS and used consistently every year, the habits and routines will become fully embedded. This will reduce cognitive load for pupils, and also streamline lessons: more time will be spent on subject content, and less on teaching the routines.

The routines are not limited to supporting science teaching: they will be still more effective the more consistently they are used across subjects. As science lead, you could consider beginning your own dialogue with other subject leads to decide school-wide strategies and routines.

Stimuli for discussion

Great dialogue can be stimulated in a variety of ways. Below are some ideas and examples of how to do this in science, which can all be used across key stages. Ideally, each science lesson would include at least one really rich stimulus for discussion, linked directly to the key learning of the lesson. The ideas could also be used to illicit what pupils already know and to identify misconceptions at the beginning of a lesson or unit, or to deepen understanding after main learning.

As a science leader, you need to support your teachers to utilise these strategies, or strategies like these, in their lessons. Ensure that they are used intentionally to promote good dialogue.

STIMULUS	EXPLANATION AND EXAMPLE
Poems and stories	Stories can be an engaging way to spark discussion and draw out misconceptions. For example, the well-known story 'The Three Little Pigs' could be used to spark discussion around the properties and suitability of different materials. This stimulus could be approached as follows. 1. Read pupils the story. 2. Pose questions for discussion: 'Why did the first pig's house blow down?' 'Which was the best material for building, and why?' 'What other materials could the pigs have tried?' 3. Prompt pupils to engage practically, building with and testing a range of materials.
Concrete resources	Before a lesson about seed dispersal, pupils could be presented with lots of different types of seed and asked to discuss their similarities and differences. You could provide prompts for comments on shape, size and texture. For example: 'Which seed is the biggest?' 'This seed feels rough. Does that one feel the same?'. This could be revisited after teaching, to see whether pupils can now classify the seeds by type of seed dispersal. For example: 'This seed is spiky, so it must attach to an animal's fur.' (Pupils love being able to interact with concrete resources, but pictures and cards can also work here.)

STIMULUS	EXPLANATION AND EXAMPLE
Demonstrations	As well as providing an opportunity for high-quality dialogue, demonstrations can really help to bring the 'wow factor' to lessons. The best demonstrations build on pupils' learning by proving a concept they have just learned. For example, in a lesson on water resistance, pupils will learn that the shape of an object affects the amount of water resistance it experiences. This concept can then be brought to life with a demonstration in which the teacher drops two differently shaped objects (perhaps made from plasticine or tin foil) through a liquid (perhaps washing-up liquid or vegetable oil, as well as water). Good demonstrations should always be coupled with a chance for discussion. For example, ask: 'What did you observe?' 'Why do you think that happened?' 'What would you like to test further?'
Concept cartoons, talking heads and talking points	Science concept cartoons (sometimes called 'talking heads') are visual representations of science ideas. These simple cartoon-style drawings put forward a range of viewpoints in contexts designed to motivate and engage pupils, and to stimulate discussion of their ideas. They are purposefully designed so that some of the viewpoints put forward are underdeveloped or incorrect, meaning they can be used to demonstrate and illicit misconceptions. Figure 10.1 below aims to stimulate discussion about evolution. **Figure 10.1:** *Concept cartoon for three statements about how cacti evolved*

STIMULUS	EXPLANATION AND EXAMPLE
	Person A is giving the most-correct answer. The statements of both Person B and Person C may draw out misconceptions about organisms being able to choose their adaptations. Concept cartoons are easy for teachers to make themselves (as simple stick people will do!) but plenty can be found online. Alternatively, lists of 'talking points' can have the same function: the contrasting statements are simply written out as text. For example, in a forces topic, you might present groups with the following list of statements for discussion. • A small object falls to the ground at the same speed as a large object. • Things stop when they run out of force. • A falling object pulled by gravity is pushed by air resistance. • A large object has more air resistance.
'What if …' questions	'What if …' questions are a great way for pupils to apply their learning at the end of a lesson or topic. For example, after being taught about the importance of plants as producers at the starts of most food chains, pupils could be asked: 'What would the world be like if there were no plants?' After learning about the function of the skeleton, pupils could be asked: 'What would your body be like if you had no bones?'
'Odd one out' activities	Pupils could be presented with a number of images, and asked which is the odd one out. The images could invite multiple correct answers, encouraging discussion skills as well as observation skills, as pupils need to justify their choices. For example, pupils could be shown three animals as follows. **Figure 10.2:** A grey wolf, a red squirrel and a deer Pupils could make their choices based on how the animals look, where they live, what they eat, their adaptations, their classification or any other factors.

Case study: using discussion stimuli

Misha is a science subject lead working in a small primary school in Harrogate. MLT and SLT recently conducted a booklook across the school. They found that the writing in science books was weak due to pupils not writing in full sentences or fully explaining their answers. This contrasted with high-quality writing in literacy books.

In her learning walks, Misha has also noticed that the quality of scientific talk from pupils is not very high. She thinks the two things may be related. She decides to tackle the talk in the classroom first, as high-quality talk is a prerequisite for high-quality writing.

She creates a bank of examples for great science discussion stimuli, and she also gets her teaching assistant to film her using these in lessons. This means teachers can see a clear model of how she extends pupil talk, and how she generates and scaffolds discussion. She introduces these ideas in a PD session.

In her learning walks in the subsequent weeks, Misha then identifies teachers who might need further support and practice.

What is 'academic talk'?

In education, the distinction between everyday talk and academic talk is too often overlooked (Quigley, 2018). Everyday talk comes naturally to most pupils. It is easier to understand and is informal in its nature. Academic talk, which we use in school science classrooms, universities and professions, is much more elaborate and complex. Neither way of talking is better than the other: they're just different tools for different situations. We can think of it as like having both casual and formal clothes in the wardrobe.

Academic talk usually needs to be specifically taught in the classroom. We also need to make it clear to pupils when they should be using which type of talk. This is especially true in science: pupils need to learn how to use precise terms and explain complex ideas clearly. Consider the contrast between these types of talk in a hypothetical classroom:

In everyday talk: When we put the metal in, we could see bubbles.
In academic talk: When the magnesium was combined with the vinegar, we observed the signs of a chemical reaction.

It's important that teachers help pupils to see the differences. Pupils then need guidance and vocabulary to adapt their talk. Practising academic talk routinely within the classroom, in both spoken word and written form, can ingrain this language as a habit.

The following table suggests some strategies teachers could use to approach this.

STRATEGY	EXPLANATION AND EXAMPLE
Modelling, including thinking out loud	It is important to model academic talk. We need to use scientific vocabulary when we are speaking in our science classrooms. We also need to draw attention to the fact that we are doing this, and explicitly teach our pupils the words they will need to do the same. For example: • A scientist would say it like this … • Here's an example of a conclusion. Which scientific key words have I used?
Enhancing word choice in pupils' answers	One way of helping students to practise academic talk is by supporting them to adjust their word choice in answers. For example: • A scientist would say 'observe' instead of 'see'. Can you try again? • Good answer. How would a scientist say that? • Can you use the word 'conclude' in your explanation? • Can you use a key word in that sentence?
Asking probing questions	Pupils need to understand that scientific talk also uses logic, reason and supporting evidence. Probing questions can prompt pupils to expand on initial responses. For example: • Can you explain your thinking with evidence? • How would you test your hypothesis? • How confident are you in your results? • Why do you think that?

Argumentation

There is a particular type of talk in the realm of science called 'argumentation'. The EEF (Holman et al., 2018) gives a comprehensive definition:

Argumentation is a specific form of dialogue that can help pupils make reasoned claims that are backed by evidence. This helps them to understand the power and limitation of scientific knowledge, showing not only what we know but how we know. (p.16)

Harlen & Qualter (2014) state that argumentation is different from a discussion or an everyday argument because it must include reasoning about whether evidence supports its conclusion. It may also consider different interpretations of evidence, and be able to identify alternative reasons for observations.

The structure of an argument can vary, but the Nuffield Foundation (2013) identified three main factors of 'claim', 'data' and 'warrants':

Claim: a statement that something is the case e.g. plants need water to survive

Data: the evidence that supports a claim e.g. the cress that was not watered withered and died

Warrants: an explanation of the data which supports your claim e.g. plants need water to make their own food

An example of a weak argument would be:

Claim: We must see because light enters the eye.

Data: You need light to see by.

Warrants: After all, otherwise we would be able to see in the dark. (Osborne et al., 2004, p. 14)

An example of a stronger argument would be:

Claim: We are able to see because light enters our eyes.

Data: We can't see when there is no light at all.

Warrants: The eye is like a camera with a light sensitive coating at the back which picks up light coming in.

It is important to scaffold and support argumentation in the science classroom, as this type of talk is a crucial part of how scientists work. If pupils can take part in academic dialogue, this is also the first step in them being able to form written conclusions to their investigations and research. Teachers can encourage argumentation by:

- teaching the parts explicitly
- modelling good arguments
- providing pupils with examples
- providing pupils with sentence stems
- showing pupils how to improve their arguments.

A simpler way of thinking about the three factors of argumentation (the claim, data and warrant) is to frame them as prompt questions. This has the benefit of using simplified language, and therefore language that can be used across primary subjects.

Claim: What have we found to be true?

Data: How does the evidence supports this?

Warrants: Why is this the case?

The following table provides examples of sentence stems that could help pupils to answer those questions.

FACTOR	PROMPT QUESTIONS
Claim: What?	- My argument is … - My prediction is … - I believe that …
Data: How?	- An example of this is … - The evidence to support my argument is … - I would convince somebody who does not believe me by … - From our experiment, you can see … - The data show that …
Warrant: Why?	- The reason for this is … - This scientific idea that explains this is … - This is explained by …

In practice: developing argumentation skills

Progression of argumentation skills from EYFS to Upper Key Stage 2 could look like the example below.

STAGE	EXAMPLE
EYFS	Pupils describe what has happened in a scientific situation. For example: • If I push this side of the see-saw, the other side will go up. • This week, our plant has grown taller. • The ice melted when we put it outside in the sun.
KS1	Pupils connect data they have gathered or observations they have made to answering questions. For example, when asked, 'Which material was the strongest?' a pupil may answer, 'Tin foil was the strongest material because it didn't break when we put the weight on it.'
Lower KS2	With scaffolding, pupils begin to form arguments with three clear parts (claim, data and warrant). For example, pupils might be given different options and asked to select the best evidence from those options to support their claim.
Upper KS2	Pupils provide clear spoken and written arguments that contain a claim, data and an explanation.

Chapter summary

- Dialogue in the classroom supports engagement and allows pupils to rehearse and develop their thinking. It can also be used by teachers to gather information about pupils' learning.
- It is important to set up specific routines that support dialogue, including ground rules, tracking, sentence stems and accountably.
- Rich science discussions can be stimulated in a wide variety of ways, including stories, concrete objects, demonstrations and concept cartoons.
- It is important for teachers to model and scaffold 'academic talk'.
- One specific type of academic talk, 'argumentation', needs to be taught explicitly. Its main factors are a claim, data and warrants.

Questions for reflection

- How do we promote dialogue and discussion in our classrooms?
- Is there an opportunity for discussion in each of our science lessons? How is this developed?
- Can our pupils explain how a scientist would talk? Can our staff?

Example PD session: developing academic talk

Here is an example of what a PD session on how to help pupils use 'academic talk' could look like.

TIMING SUGGESTION	SESSION GUIDANCE
Before the session	Ask teachers to bring their lesson plans for the next week.
5 mins	Give teachers direct instruction on the differences between 'everyday talk' and 'academic talk', providing examples.
5 mins	Model strategies for how to help pupils adapt their talk. For suggestions, refer to the table in the section of this chapter titled 'What is 'academic talk'?'
15 mins	- Ask teachers to look at their upcoming lessons, and to script expected pupil responses (in everyday talk) and then their responses to prompt academic talk. - Ask them to practice in pairs, giving each other feedback.
5 mins	Give teachers direct instruction on what argumentation is, providing examples. Discuss what progression looks like across key stages, referring to the table in the 'Developing argumentation skills' section of this chapter.
15 mins	- Give teachers a range of scientific questions and ask them to write an argument in response to each one. - Ask them to swap answers with partners, and to identify the three parts of the argument (the claim, data and warrants) in each answer.

Explore further

- The EEF's *Improving Secondary Science Guidance Report* (2018) by Sir John Holman and Emily Yeomans: https://d2tic4wvo1iusb.cloudfront.net/production/eef-guidance-reports/science-ks3-ks4/Secondary-Science-v2.96-WEB.pdf?v=1737382009 (see Recommendation 2)
- *Starting a lesson with Initial Stimulus Material* (2017) by Harry Fletcher Wood: https://improvingteaching.co.uk/2017/01/15/starting-a-lesson-with-initial-stimulus-material/
- The Lawrence Hall of Science's *The Argumentation Toolkit* resources: https://argumentationtoolkit.lawrencehallofscience.org/
- Impact's *Promoting student-led questions in the secondary science classroom* (2021) by Adewale Magaji
- The Association of Science Education's Developing talk in the primary science classroom (2020) by Jo Moore

11 Disciplinary literacy

Strong, consistent correlations between pupils' literacy skills and their success in learning science have been demonstrated clearly by the EEF (Quigley et al., 2021). Literacy interventions, furthermore, have shown considerable impacts on science outcomes. This is, perhaps, unsurprising when we consider that literacy is fundamental to both understanding written scientific texts and expressing ideas about science.

Literacy skills (spoken language, vocabulary, reading and writing) are both general and subject-specific. They are general in that reading fluently benefits pupils across the curriculum. They are subject-specific in that each subject has its own unique language, ways of doing and styles of communicating. For example, a historian would write differently to a scientist.

Disciplinary literacy is an approach to cross-curricular literacy that involves teaching the specifics of reading, writing and communicating in a discipline (Quigley et al., 2021). In science, this means teaching pupils about the factors that make language and literature unique in science: teaching them how to read, write and verbally communicate like scientists (Moje, 2008; Shanahan & Shanahan, 2008; 2012).

This chapter's focus is on disciplinary literacy in scientific reading and writing, both relating to and contrasting with the focuses on vocabulary and dialogue in Chapters 8 and 10. The science disciplinary literacy requirements for EYFS and Key Stage 1 centre on those skills categories. There, they develop the oracy that lays the foundations for great science literacy. This chapter, therefore, is relevant mostly to the Key Stage 2 curriculum.

The chapter will cover:

- what makes reading and writing in science distinct from other disciplines
- the importance of providing an array of scientific texts for pupils to read and explore
- the components that are characteristic of science writing
- ways to guide composition of explanation texts and investigation reports.

Disciplinary literacy in science

As a science leader, you need to be aware of the characteristics of language and literacy in science that make it distinct from other subjects. For example, historical texts are written in a style remarkably different from that of scientific reports: in history, disciplinary literacy involves reading and writing that concentrates on sources' context and corroboration. In physical education, it could focus on providing feedback to peers by clearly describing their performance using technical vocabulary (Quigley et al., 2021). In science, contrastingly, it involves formulating and describing methods, explanations and conclusions.

Key features of the language of science

Noun-heavy

Science uses particularly noun-centric language: approximately 60% of the words in science texts are nouns (Biber & Gray, 2017). Nominalisation (turning verbs into nouns) is common. For example, 'the water evaporates' is more often expressed as 'evaporation occurs'; 'the chemicals reacted and bubbles formed' becomes 'the chemical reaction resulted in the formation of bubbles'.

The passive voice

The passive voice is common. It places focus on the object of an action rather than the subject, usually positioning the object noun at the beginning of a sentence. Effectively, it emphasises a result rather than who or what caused it. The subject may not be identified at all. For example:

ACTIVE VOICE	PASSIVE VOICE
Scientists classify glass as a solid.	Glass is classified as a solid.
The plant absorbed water through its roots.	Water was absorbed by the plant through its roots.

Scientists use the passive voice to remove the focus from the researcher, making writing more impersonal and formal.

Limited focus on authors

As use of the passive voice suggests, the importance of a science text's author is limited. This contrasts with the vital importance of historical texts' sources: historians consider, 'Who is the author? What biases might they have? How does this influence my interpretation?' Conversely, scientists think about the author primarily for vetting purposes: 'With what laboratory is this author affiliated? Is their work credible?' After this initial vetting, scientists can disregard the author's identity and focus on the content (Haynes, 2020). Any opinions expressed are, generally, hindrances.

Multi-modal expression

Science naturally involves multiple ways of presenting information (Lemke, 2004): knowledge can usually be explained in several different modes. For example, the water cycle can be described with words, shown with diagrams (both illustrative scenes and flow charts), and summarised with mathematical formulas that help to make predictions. Presenting new scientific knowledge to pupils in several different ways can aid understanding.

Drawing attention to scientific language features

Pupils will encounter these science-specific language features through the spoken and written content of their science lessons. However, unless we draw their attention to them, pupils are unlikely to notice. Teachers will need to point out these differences and teach them explicitly.

This could be done in different ways. Teachers could make live corrections: for example, if a pupil gives a verbal answer in the active voice, the teacher could explain that scientists normally use the passive voice and model how to edit their contribution. They could also plan in advance when they will explicitly teach a skill such as nominalisation, and give pupils a chance to apply it to a scientific explanation written in the lesson.

Reading science-specific texts

As science leaders, we also need to ensure pupils are exposed to a wide range of science-specific texts, are taught strategies for comprehending these and become familiar with their features.

Pupils should have the chance to read authentic science books and journal articles, but it is important that these are at an age-appropriate level (Holman et al., 2018). At a primary level, appropriate texts are much more likely to include science news articles, information texts and non-fiction class reading material. We can support our pupils in understanding the texts they read by explicitly teaching them the vocabulary they will need, and by supporting comprehension through structured activities.

Here are some ideas for how to do this. Below is a table (adapted from Osborne and Dillon, 2010) that suggests different types of Directed Activities Related to Text (DARTs).

RECONSTRUCTION DARTs	ANALYSIS DARTs
Completing text, diagrams or tables: • Completing phrases or sentences • Labelling diagrams using text • Using text to complete tables	Marking and labelling: • Searching for and underlining specified parts of texts • Labelling text with supplied labels • Segmenting text and labelling the different parts
Ordering and classifying text: • Putting segments of text into a logical order • Classifying segments of text according to set categories (such as instructions, explanations and evidence)	Recording and constructing: • Constructing diagrams to show the content and flow of texts • Creating tables from information in texts • Using texts to answer or create questions • Listing the key points made in texts
Predicting: • Writing the next parts of texts	

Providing access to scientific texts

As science leaders, we need to make sure that, as young as possible, our pupils have access and are exposed to non-fiction science texts and books, alongside stories and fiction. Engaging young learners with scientific texts offers exciting opportunities to deepen their understanding, and to spark curiosity.

This starts with school libraries and classroom book corners. We want to create inviting classroom reading spaces that include carefully curated collections of science books. For Key Stage 1, you could display picture-rich texts such as Louie Stowell's *Look Inside Your Body* alongside narrative non-fiction like the *One Day on Our Blue Planet* series by Ella Bailey. For Key Stage 2, include more-challenging texts like *Science Year by Year* by Robert Winston, and Andrea Mills's *100 Scientists Who Made History*.

You'll also need to plan time in lessons for pupils to read these texts, with the guidance of their teachers, and for them to engage in some of the activities suggested above. During science lessons, pupils could be given the opportunity to explore texts that reinforce recently taught concepts. For example, after a Y2 lesson on plant growth, pupils might read *A Seed Grows* by Pamela Hickman. This would help them to make connections between their hands-on observations and the extra insight provided by the book's detailed illustrations.

I am not advocating that new learning in science is introduced to pupils primarily through text: teachers are able to teach new content much more effectively through direct instruction. However, once new content has been taught, it is certainly a worthwhile exercise for pupils to encounter that knowledge in their reading. It will sometimes be appropriate to include this in a lesson, but it can also be done elsewhere. For example, science books and stories could be shared in English, during story time or reading lessons. In Key Stage 1, for instance, pupils could read engaging narratives like Andrea Beaty's *Ada Twist, Scientist* to inspire scientific thinking. Y4 pupils might analyse *The Extraordinary Life of Katherine Johnson* by Devika Jina, connecting it to their space topic while developing comprehension skills.

Writing scientifically

Good science writing includes many of the elements of general good writing, plus some additional specific skills and approaches. This section of the chapter will first set out some key foundational writing skills that will be as important to science as any other subject. It will then consider how these apply to science practically, and what else is needed.

Writing is a complex process, which requires explicit instruction in and careful development of multiple skills. It encompasses several key components, including (but not limited to) fine motor skills, handwriting, spelling, composition, vocabulary, grammar and punctuation. Due to the complexity of the process, the cognitive load incurred by a writing task is much larger than that by an oral contribution.

Teachers can support writing through various strategies (adapted from Quigley et al., 2021). They can:

- use pre-writing activities to ensure pupils have secure background knowledge and vocabulary related to the topic
- provide instruction at word, sentence and whole-text levels

- gradually reduce support and scaffolding to support pupils' growing independence
- sequence talk activities alongside reading and writing tasks, practising new vocabulary and developing ideas
- use sentence starters and prompts to help pupils structure and extend their responses
- provide high-quality models
- use metacognitive instruction: demonstrations of the writing process that include consistent narration of thought processes regarding structure and sentence composition.

Composing explanations and information texts

What types of writing might our pupils be expected to do in their primary science lessons? Firstly, we might require them to communicate their learning and ideas about science in longer answer questions. For example, we might expect a Key Stage 2 pupil to write a short paragraph on how polar bears are adapted to their environments.

Later, we might plan for pupils to compose extended pieces of writing. For example, we might ask them to write information texts on how the digestive system works. We would expect pieces like these to include common features of information texts, such a labelled diagrams and subheadings.

Neither of these types of writing is specific to science lessons. Pupils are expected to write narratives, including non-fiction, across the curriculum, but we want to ensure our pupils include the disciplinary elements common in science writing, like passive voice and nominalisation (as covered in the 'Disciplinary literacy in science' section above). Exercises including these are useful: they not only support literacy across the curriculum, but also provide opportunities for pupils to practise writing like a scientist. This, in turn, provides more opportunities for learning: when pupils write about science, they reflect on their understanding, formulate their ideas and combine ideas in new ways.

Investigation reports

The type of subject-specific writing most common in primary science is the investigation report, in which where pupils explain an investigation they conducted. This is a type of writing that pupils will also be expected to complete at secondary level, and it mirrors how career scientists write up and publish experimental research. The main parts of an investigation reports are as follows.

1. Title or investigation question
2. Equipment list and method
3. Results
4. Conclusion

Pupils will learn about proposing and rejecting or accepting hypotheses as they progress into secondary school, but that is not necessary at primary level. It is likely that pupils will need to draw scientific diagrams, though, to show how to set up equipment and/or as part of their results.

Case study: improving science writing

Marcia is a primary science lead at a school in Doncaster. While doing a book-looks, she notices that the standard of science writing is much higher in Y4 than in Y5. The scientific conclusions in Y4 are much more fit for purpose, containing evidence and well-explained points. In Y5, scientific experiments seem mostly to be written up in a narrative style, like diary entries.

Marcia speaks to the Y5 teacher who plans science, and realises that he isn't clear about how good science writing should look. Marcia reflects that this is not laid out anywhere in the curriculum they use. She can see why teachers may have ended up teaching quite different writing styles.

Marcia starts to address the problem by thinking about the end point that she wants her pupils to reach in Y6. She writes some model examples of experiment write-ups and conclusions. She then annotates these models to produce a set of success criteria.

Marcia then holds a PD session in which she presents these model end points to teachers. Together, they come up with granular criteria for how progression could look in each year group.

Results

Results can be presented in a variety of ways, from diagrams to tables, to graphs, to pie charts. As a general rule of thumb, pupils should be asked to present data only in ways they have already learned and consolidated in maths lessons. Otherwise, pupils' cognitive load shifts away from learning the science you want to teach, and towards trying to understand new statistical methods.

To ensure this, it is worth reviewing the maths curriculum. You could even set up a meeting with your school's maths leader to ensure that your curriculums align, and to look for opportunities for maths learning to be reinforced in science lessons in each year group.

You could also consider whether some elements of an experiment's review could be explained verbally. I do not expect my pupils to write up a full investigation report every time they do an experiment. Sometimes we will just focus in on one part of a report, depending on how much time we have in the lesson, or where pupils need more practice.

Scientific methods

The purpose of a scientific method is to provide a set of instructions so other scientists could replicate the experiment. These should be clear and concise.

Pupils should be provided with model examples of good scientific methods, and sharing non-examples can also be a useful exercise. Pupils should additionally be provided with success criteria for writing a clear method.

In practice: teaching a non-example

The first time I teach about scientific methods I like to give my pupils an unclear set of instructions and watch them all experience the limitation themselves as they struggle to get to the desired end point. For example, I may give them a piece of paper and ask them to fold it twice, then fold it in half, then fold it four times. I then show them the photo shown in Figure 11.1 and surprise, surprise no one's folding has ever matched the intended outcome. We then reflect on the method together and suggest ways of improving it and making the instructions more specific.

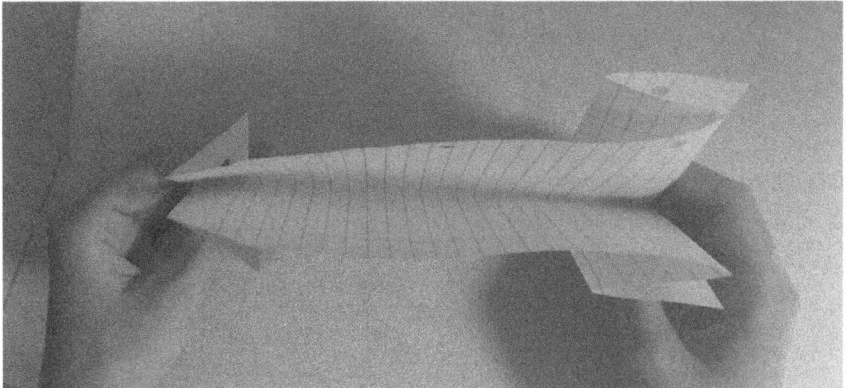

Figure 11.1: intended outcome for folding paper

In practice: success criteria for writing clear instructions

Below are the success criteria I use with my pupils for writing clear instructions for the method in a science report.

- Underlined subheadings for 'equipment' and 'method'
- An equipment list
- Numbered instructions
- Imperative verbs
- Adverbs of time (e.g. first, next, immediately)
- Adverbs of manner (e.g. slowly, carefully)

In practice: a model experiment write-up

Let's imagine a Y3 teacher has been teaching a unit on the life cycle of plants. They've set up an experiment to focus on germination. Here is a model for a scientific method that pupils could write in that lesson:

Germination in plants

Equipment

- seed tray
- seed compost

- tomato seeds
- water

Method
1. First, fill the seed tray with seed compost.
2. Next, add water to moisten the surface of the compost.
3. Sprinkle the seeds evenly over the compost.
4. Carefully, place the seed tray in a warm place.
5. Spray the seeds with water once a day.

Chapter summary

- Literacy skills can be general (transferable across subjects) or disciplinary (specific to particular subjects).
- Disciplinary literacy in science is literacy regarding science's own unique language features and ways of communicating. It needs to be taught explicitly.
- Scientific writing's distinct characteristics include nominalisation, the passive voice, limited focus on authors and multi-modal presentation of information (including text, diagrams and formulas).
- Teachers should expose pupils to authentic science texts, including news articles, information texts and non-fiction narrative books.
- Structured activities such as DARTs can support comprehension.
- Strategies for teaching writing across the curriculum, such as metacognitive instruction, remain relevant for writing in science.
- Primary science writing includes communicating ideas, explaining learning, writing information texts, and creating investigation reports.
- Investigation reports should feature specific components, including a title, clear method, results and a conclusion.

Questions for reflection

- How does my current approach to teaching disciplinary literacy compare to the ideas presented in this chapter?
- How could I ensure that the unique characteristics of scientific writing are taught to our pupils explicitly, improving their scientific literacy?
- Consider the reading materials available to pupils. To what extent do they include varied age-appropriate science texts?
- How can we balance explicit writing instruction in science with the time constraints of covering required science content?

Example PD session: teaching disciplinary literacy

Here is an example of what a PD session on how to develop pupils' science literacy could look like.

TIMING SUGGESTION	SESSION GUIDANCE
Before the session	- Prepare copies of the school science curriculum. - Ask teachers to bring their plans for an upcoming unit of work.
10 mins	Use the introduction to this chapter to present the concept of science disciplinary literacy. Specifically, discuss the research evidence linking science attainment to literacy skills.
5 mins	Use the 'Reading science-specific texts' section of this chapter to focus discussion on the importance of reading varied science texts.
15 mins	Go through the different categories of DARTs, finding an example from the science curriculum that would be appropriate for each one.
20 mins	- Ask teachers to look through their plans and incorporate a relevant DART activity that could support each learning point. - Ask teachers to share their activity ideas in pairs, and to give each other feedback on the planning.

Explore further

- Arc (State of Victoria Department of Education)'s *Literacy Teaching Toolkit*: https://arc.educationapps.vic.gov.au/learning/sites/literacy
- *Writing Revolution Activities in Primary Science* (2018) by Tarjinder Gill: https://www.teach-well.com/writing-revolution-activities-in-primary-science/
- *Reading and Writing in Science: Tools to Develop Disciplinary Literacy* (2009) by Maria Grant and Douglas Fisher
- *The Writing Revolution: A Guide to Advanced Thinking* (2024) by Judith C. Hochman and Natalie Wexler
- The EEF's *Improving Literacy in Secondary Schools Guidance Report* (2021) by Alex Quigley and Robbie Coleman
- *Disciplinary Literacy in the Primary School* (2019) by Timothy Shanahan: https://ncca.ie/media/4679/disciplinary-literacy-in-the-primary-school-professor-timothy-shanahan-university-of-illinois-at-chicago-1.pdf
- *How Talk for Writing Supports Science* (2024) by Julia Strong and Pie Corbett
- *The Art and Science of Teaching Primary Reading* (2021) by Christopher Such

12 Engagement in science

> Pupil engagement – their interest and, hence, their motivation – is crucial for learning. Research has shown that it leads to more positive outcomes for pupils: improved attainment, increased attendance, improved wellbeing and protection against risky behaviours (Skinner et al., 2008; Howard et al., 2021). We know that learning requires effort, concentration and discipline, so it's not surprising that pupils are more likely to give up if they are not motivated. Being sufficiently curious and excited about what you're learning can make the effort involved in learning seem worthwhile.
>
> Engagement is important for us to consider as science leads: ultimately, we want our pupils to be interested and successful in science, at school and beyond. It is important to note, though, that engagement is not a proxy for learning itself. A pupil could have high levels of interest and enjoyment in a task, but not actually learn anything from it. They could watch and appreciate a science cartoon, for example, but then not be able to recall its core content.
>
> Nevertheless, a thorough understanding of pupil engagement can benefit you, your teachers and your pupils alike. In this chapter, we will cover:
>
> - the concept of science capital, why it is important and how we can increase it
> - the importance of diversity in the curriculum
> - the power of storytelling and citizen science for improving engagement.

Science capital

The concept of science capital can help us to understand why some people engage with science and others do not, considering all the science-related resources a person may have. It was developed during the ASPIRES project

(2020), a ten-year longitudinal study of young people's science and career aspirations.

Science capital can be imagined as a metaphorical bag that holds all of an individual's science-related interests, knowledge, attitudes, experiences and social contacts. This bag can be divided into four main 'pockets':

- Knowledge: What you know about science (scientific knowledge, literacy and understanding)
- Attitudes: How you think about science (science-related impressions and dispositions)
- Experiences: Science-related activities you do (such as reading journal articles or visiting science exhibits)
- Social contacts: People who talk about science with you (such as a sister with physics degree or a family friend repairing a vehicle)

It's important to note that science capital is not fixed: its value and potential can change, depending on context. For example, a pupil may have science-related interests, skills and experiences that go unnoticed in the classroom but are highly valuable in other settings.

Growing science capital is important for several reasons (Nag Chowdhuri et al., 2021): it promotes diversity in STEM fields, it contributes to a scientifically literate population and it encourages aspirations to study science further. Vitally, it also enhances pupil engagement. Pupils with higher science capital tend to find science more relevant to their lives, and are more likely to engage with the subject in meaningful ways.

Improving pupils' science capital

To help more – and more diverse – pupils to engage with science, a science-capital teaching approach first and foremost builds on good teaching practice. This is how we can grow capital in the first of the concept's four pockets: knowledge about science.

Good teaching practice is also inclusive, allowing all pupils to succeed and see the relevance of the curriculum to their lives. We want to influence pupils so that they can see themselves as someone 'sciencey', capable of achieving well in science and being a scientist in the future. This is a way in which teachers can affect the second science-capital pocket: attitudes to science.

Good classroom teaching alone, though, is often not sufficient for improving attitudes, or for improving experiences and social contacts. This often requires additional strategies. So let's take a look at how we, as science leads, can do this!

Here are some strategies based on the Primary Science Capital Teaching Approach (Nag Chowdhuri et al., 2021). The sources suggested for furthering ideas can also be found in the 'Explore further' section at the end of this chapter.

POCKET	IDEAS TO BUILD SCIENCE CAPITAL	SUGGESTED SOURCES
Attitudes	• Link everyday teaching to experiences in pupils' own lives. • Cultivate the idea that science skills, and science qualifications, are transferable and useful in many areas of life, not just science-based careers.	Explorify's activities link science learning to everyday life and aim to cultivate transferrable problem-solving skills.
Experiences	• Use homework and project work to encourage pupils to engage in science-related activities outside school. • Introduce pupils to relevant and appropriate science-related media (such as TV programmes, online resources, books and magazines). • Enable to take part in local science learning opportunities and trips.	• The Royal Institution suggests home-project ideas and provides grants for science shows. • Twig Science Reporter is a great children's science-news site.
Social contacts	• Help pupils to recognise the broad range of scientific knowledge that already exists in their families, local communities and school (such as an interest in gardening). • Connect pupils with people who use science at work, ideally through repeated interactions (virtually or in person).	STEM Learning's ambassadors programme can be used to arrange visits from scientists who can host a range of school activities.

> ### Case study: a subject lead example
>
> Hakeem is a science subject lead working in a primary school in Essex. While analysing the end-of-term grades from the previous academic year, he notices that there are clear gender discrepancies across most year groups: boys are repeatedly outperforming girls.
>
> Hakeem wants to explore this further, so he conducts some pupil-voice sessions. Both boys and girls expressed enjoyment in science, but far more boys stated that they would be interested in science-related careers such as engineering, medicine and aeronautics.
>
> Hakeem knows that there could be links between pupils' science capital, their motivation and therefore their academic success in science, so he decides to gather more data. He uses a template from the PSCTA's to hold a survey of pupil's science-capital levels. It confirms his findings that there are clear gender discrepancies in science capital.
>
> Hakeem decides to create a science-capital action plan for the next academic year. He decides on four main targets:
>
> - Each year group will have a science-related trip or experience in the local community.
> - The school will organise a school-wide science fair.
> - The science department will run a STEM club for girls.
> - The school will organise a science careers event including a visit from at least one female scientist.
>
> At the end of the academic year he will re-run the pupil science capital survey to see if there have been any changes to the science capital of all pupils.

A diverse range of scientists

Ultimately, we want every pupil to believe that they *could* be a scientist, and representation is a big part of that. If pupils are not shown that all types of people can be successful in science careers, they may be less likely to see themselves as a scientist in the future. By including a diverse range of scientists in our curriculums, making sure our resources are inclusive and ensuring any visiting speakers reflect the diversity of our pupil populations.

It is vital that, as educators, we challenge pervasive stereotypes about scientists. One simple step I would urge all teachers to take is to think about the stock images you might use in your lessons. Generally, search engines produce images of white male scientists: it's both easy and important to widen your search and ensure that all your pupils are represented in the images you display.

Diversity should also be taken into consideration when planning your curriculum. Does that mean we exclude white males? Of course not. It is nearly impossible to teach evolution without mentioning Charles Darwin, electricity without Edison or gravity without Newton. These scientists have become synonymous with their discoveries and areas of expertise, so they are included in curriculums without much conscious thought. In order to complement them with a more-diverse range of scientists, a bit more conscious thought and forward planning is required.

Below is a list of scientists, including the 'big names', who could feature in your curriculums.

TOPIC	SCIENTIST	ROLES AND SELECT ACHIEVEMENTS
Plants	Joseph Banks (1743–1820)	Botanist and explorer • Discovered and documented plants from all around the world (travelling with James Cook) • Worked to keep scientists in contact during wars
	Margaret Rebecca Dickinson (1821–1918)	Botanist and painter • Painted detailed images of British plants that are now used as historical records
	Marianne North (1830–1890)	Botanist and painter • Painted detailed images of plants from all over the world, used by experts including Charles Darwin
	George Washington Carver (1864–1943)	Botanist and inventor • Pioneered crop rotation • Discovered over 300 uses for peanuts
	Beatrix Potter (1866–1943)	Botanist, painter and writer • Made discoveries about microscopic elements of fungi and how they reproduced
	Percy L. Julian (1899–1975)	Biochemist • Developed medicines from plants

TOPIC	SCIENTIST	ROLES AND SELECT ACHIEVEMENTS
Living things and their habitats	Maria Sibylla Merian (1647–1717)	Entomologist and illustrator • Made discoveries about insects' life cycles, including how caterpillars become butterflies
	Carl Linnaeus (1707–1778)	Botanist, physician and zoologist • Came up with the system for naming and classifying living organisms that we use today
	Charles Darwin (1809–1882)	Naturalist, geologist and biologist Developed the theory of evolution by natural selection
	Charles Henry Turner (1867–1923)	Zoologist and entomologist • Discovered that insects can hear, and that honeybees can recognise colours and patterns
	Rachel Carson (1907–1964)	Marine biologist, writer and conservationist • Studied effects of pesticides • Published research that led to DDT being banned
	Eugenie Clark (1922–2015)	Marine biologist • Made so many discoveries about sharks that she was nicknamed 'the shark lady' • Pioneered use of scuba diving for research
	Jane Goodall (1934–present)	Primatologist, ethologist and anthropologist • Studies chimps and how they communicate • Works to promote non-human rights
	Sylvia Earle (1935–present)	Marine biologist, explorer and aquanaut • Explores and documents the oceans • Works to save oceans from pollution and overfishing

TOPIC	SCIENTIST	ROLES AND SELECT ACHIEVEMENTS
Materials and chemistry	Leizu, also known as Xi Ling-shi (27th century BCE)	Chinese empress • Credited with discovering how to produce silk from silkworms, a process leading to great wealth in ancient China
	Jabir ibn Hayyan (8th–9th centuries CE)	Researcher and inventor • Wrote the oldest-known scientific texts on chemistry, cosmology, astronomy, medicine, pharmacology, zoology and botany • Invented distillation and many other core chemistry processes
	Charles Macintosh (1766–1843)	Chemist and inventor • Invented a rubberised fabric to make the modern waterproof raincoat: the Mackintosh
	Alice Ball (1892–1916)	Chemist and inventor • Developed a trustworthy way to treat leprosy
	Walter Lincoln Hawkins (1911–1992)	Chemist and engineer • Invented a type of plastic to coat telephone wires, making it possible for them to reach anyone
	Ruth Benerito (1916–2013)	Chemist and inventor • Invented a way of coating fabric to make wrinkle-free cotton
	Stephanie Kwolek (1923–2014)	Chemist • Invented flame-resistant fibres to make Kevlar, which is five times stronger than steel and used in tyres, aeroplanes and bullet-proof vests

TOPIC	SCIENTIST	ROLES AND SELECT ACHIEVEMENTS
Light	Ibn al-Haitham (10th–11th centuries CE)	Mathematician, astronomer and physicist • Realised that light travels into the eye when we see • Invented the pin-hole camera
	Patricia Bath (1942–2019)	Ophthalmologist and inventor • Invented laser that could remove cataracts • Started community outreach eye-care programmes
	Liz West (1985–present)	Artist • Uses light to explore colour, creating installations for museums and science centres
Human health	Charles R. Drew (1904–1950)	Surgeon and medical researcher • Invented the blood bank
	Asima Chatterjee (1917–2006)	Chemist • Developed early ways to treat epilepsy and malaria
	Marie Maynard Daly (1921–2003)	Biochemist • Researched proteins in a way that helped breakthroughs about DNA • Made discoveries about the effects of chemicals, including cholesterol and sugar, on the heart
	Tu Youyou (1930–present)	Chemist • Developed groundbreaking modern ways to treat malaria • Won a Nobel Prize and Lasker Award in Medicine
	Nancy Chang (1950–present)	Biochemist • Developed ways to treat asthma, allergies and HIV/AIDS

TOPIC	SCIENTIST	ROLES AND SELECT ACHIEVEMENTS
Rocks	Mary Anning (1799–1847)	Fossil collector and palaeontologist • Found extraordinary fossils that led to understanding of dinosaurs, including the first complete ichthyosaur skeleton fossil
	Katia & Maurice Krafft (1942–1991) (1946–1991)	Volcanologists and filmmakers • Pioneered photographic study of volcanic eruptions and reducing their risks
Earth and Space	Ptolemy 100–170 CE	Mathematician, astronomer and geographer • Promoted the (disproved) geocentric theory of the universe • Created the first global coordinate system (lines of latitude and longitude) on a hugely influential early world map
	Copernicus (1473–1543)	Mathematician and astronomer • Pioneered the heliocentric theory of the universe
	Caroline Herschel (1750–1848)	Astronomer and mathematician • First woman to discover a comet • First woman to hold office in English government
	Wang Zhenyi (1768–1797)	Astronomer, poet and mathematician • Promoted the idea that Earth is a sphere • Explained eclipses
	Katherine Johnson (1918–2020)	Physicist and mathematician • Led mathematical work at NASA that led to manned missions in space, including the Moon landing • Pioneered use of computers for mathematics at NASA
	Valentina Tereshkova (1937–present)	Engineer and cosmonaut • Was the first woman in space
	Mae Jemison (1956–present)	Engineer, physician and astronaut • Was the first African-American woman in space
	Helen Sharman (1963–present)	Chemist and cosmonaut • Was the first British person in space

TOPIC	SCIENTIST	ROLES AND SELECT ACHIEVEMENTS
Forces	Galileo Galilei (1564–1642)	Astronomer, physicist and engineer • Made discoveries about speed, gravity and motion • Invented early telescopes, microscopes, compasses and thermometers • Made discoveries about the solar system
	Isaac Newton (1642–1727)	Mathematician, physicist and astronomer • Refined theories about speed, gravity and motion • Made accurate predictions about the movement of Earth and other planets
	Stephen Hawking (1942–2018)	Theoretical physicist and cosmologist • Made discoveries about the structure of the universe, the Big Bang and black holes • Developed theories about quantum mechanics
Electricity	Michael Faraday (1791–1867)	Chemist and physicist • Made discoveries about electromagnets • Discovered that magnetism can affect light
	Thomas Edison (1847–1931)	Inventor • Invented gramophones, movie cameras incandescent light bulbs
	Lewis Howard Latimer (1848–1928)	Inventor • Invented carbon filament for incandescent lightbulbs • Improved technology for train lavatories and early air conditioners
	Hertha Ayrton (1854–1923)	Engineer, mathematician, physicist and inventor • Improved electric arc lighting • Was the first female member of the the Institution of Electrical Engineers
	Nicolas Tesla (1856–1943)	Engineer, physicist and inventor • Invented early X-ray imaging • Made discoveries about wireless energy transfer
	James West (1931–present)	Inventor • Developed technology for microphones, to become used in devices including telephones, camcorders and hearing aids

Citizen research projects

A great way to help show that science is relevant to pupils' lives, to foster engagement and to build practical skills is by finding opportunities for pupils to take part in real scientific research projects that contribute to the work of scientists around the world. This involvement can take various forms, such as gathering new data or examining and interpreting existing information.

Many of these projects align directly with school curriculums, making them valuable educational tools. The most significant advantage for young learners goes beyond just curriculum connections, though. By engaging in real, ongoing scientific studies, pupils gain first-hand experience of understanding the purposes and methods of scientific research. This practical involvement helps them to grasp the 'how' and 'why' behind scientific investigations, fostering a deeper appreciation of the scientific process.

Below are some examples.

PROJECT	DESCRIPTION
What's Under Your Feet?	This project is run by the British Trust for Ornithology and EDF Energy. It invites pupils to dig up small soil samples and count the number of earthworms and other larger invertebrates living in the soil. By repeating these surveys three times a year, the project aims to help scientists understand how climate changes are impacting invertebrate populations – which, in turn, affect bird numbers and migration patterns in different areas.
Wildwatch Kenya	Scientists from the San Diego Zoo are collaborating with conservation experts in Kenya to study threatened wildlife, especially giraffes, in northern Kenya. They have set up motion-activated cameras across the savannah, capturing over a million images that now need to be analysed and classified. Pupils can follow a simple tutorial to start identifying the wildlife in these images, which helps the research team better understand the populations of these threatened species.
The Great British Bee Count	This citizen science project is organised by Friends of the Earth. It invites participants of all skill levels to report their sightings of bees and other pollinating insects. These observations will help scientists gain a better understanding of bee populations, and therefore which species need protection. The 'Flower-Insect Timed Count' is a quick and easy way for beginners to survey the pollinators in their local areas, without needing to identify specific species.

PROJECT	DESCRIPTION
Big Schools' Birdwatch	This annual citizen science project from the Royal Society for the Protection of Birds allows pupils to study the changing populations of British birds. Participants spend an hour observing and recording the birds they see, using a downloadable identification guide. The results are then submitted for analysis, contributing to the annual report on bird population trends. Schools can sign up for the newsletter to stay informed about the next Birdwatch event.
Zooniverse	This platform hosts a variety of citizen science projects in which members of the public can contribute to research efforts. For example, pupils can help to count iguanas in drone photographs to support conservation efforts. Projects are updated regularly.
Nature's Calendar	Organised by the Woodland Trust, this project invites the public to upload their observations of natural events in their local areas, such as the progression of seasonal changes. Pupils can contribute their own outdoor observations, which are then plotted on maps alongside records from across the UK. This helps to build a comprehensive database of the natural world's seasonal cycle.
Met Office Weather Observations Website	On the Met Office Weather Observations website, pupils can contribute to the understanding of climate change by entering weather observations from their local areas. This helps scientists build a rich, reliable dataset they can use to track changes over time.

Storytelling

Storytelling, perhaps the oldest form of teaching, is a powerful tool that can significantly enhance engagement and understanding in science education. Science isn't just about equations, definitions and abstract ideas: it's about real people, discoveries and the human journey of understanding our world. Stories have a unique capacity to make abstract scientific concepts more concrete and accessible.

When teachers incorporate stories into their lessons, they make science relatable and human. This approach helps pupils to see science not as a distant, impersonal subject, but as a vibrant, ongoing narrative of human curiosity and discovery. By weaving scientific principles into stories, teachers can provide context and relevance, helping pupils grasp how these ideas apply to real-world situations.

Moreover, storytelling in science education capitalises on what cognitive psychologist Daniel Willingham (2009) calls the 'psychologically privileged' status of stories in human memory. Our brains have adapted to recall stories readily, making them an excellent vehicle for teaching and learning. When scientific information is presented within a narrative structure, pupils are more likely to remember and understand the content (Bower & Clark, 1969).

By harnessing the power of narrative, teachers can make science more accessible, memorable, and engaging. Stories that link to your science learning can be used in lessons in a number of ways. For example:

- Teachers could start each unit or lesson with a story. This story might be about a scientist who links to the topic, or feature a problem that needs to be solved (for example: 'Mr Em's umbrella has a hole in it. How are we going to fix it?')
- Pupils could retell a story after hearing it, or tell the story of their experiment after completing it.
- Pupils could draw stories about their learning using comic strips.
- Stories that link to the science topic could be shared outside of lesson time, giving pupils more time to revisit scientific content in different contexts.

Sourcing stories

So, where do we find these stories? There are several approaches to take, including:

- making links with well-known stories
- finding purpose-made science stories that someone else has written
- creating stories ourselves.

Making links with well-known stories

One benefit of using stories with which pupils are already familiar is that it reduces some cognitive load. It also makes the learning more relevant to them and their prior experiences.

Lots of well-known tales could be linked to science topics. For example, *The Three Little Pigs* links very well to the Key Stage 1 topic of materials: pupils could test out different materials to build houses, experimenting to see which is the strongest. You could also consider:

- linking *Jack and the Beanstalk* to the topic of Plants
- linking *The Princess and the Pea* to topics involving testing materials
- linking *The Billy Goats Gruff* to building and testing structures for a bridge
- linking *The Gingerbread Man* to activities that experiment with floating and sinking.

These work particularly well with EYFS and Key Stage 1, as this is often the age that pupils engage most with these types of stories. In Key Stage 2 it could work just as well with linking the science to a book they will all know well, such as a book you've studied in class. For example, if your class has read 'Iron man' by Ted Hughes, then this could be linked to magnetic materials or changes of state investigations.

Finding science stories

There are some great purpose-made science stories that can also be used. 'Science Through Stories' (also cited in the 'Explore further' section at the end of this chapter) is a good resource for this. They provide engaging science stories that link to every topic in the National Curriculum for England, along with ideas for lesson planning. You could also do some research of your own to find stories that fit the topics you will teach. Simply browsing in libraries and bookshops is a good place to start, but there are also book lists available online. The website 'Books for Topics' is a good place to start (and is also cited in the 'Explore further' section). You can also search by topic in lots of distributors' websites.

Creating stories

Sometimes, the quickest and most-effective way to tell a fun, relevant story is to create one yourself. This way, you can ensure the story fits well with the learning you want to draw out. These stories don't always have to be elaborate. For example, you might tell the story of a boy who loved football and his hunt for the perfect football boots. This story could be used as a starter for an investigation into friction on different surfaces, and is likely to feel relevant and relatable to many of your pupils.

When crafting your own stories, it can be useful to use Willingham's 4Cs as a guideline (2009).

- Character: Good stories have strong characters.
- Causality: Events in a story should connect, so one thing causes another.

- Conflict: Stories very often include difficulties or challenges that need to be overcome.
- Complications: Sub-plots (and so sub-problems) can add interest.

Including these features makes a story interesting as well as easy to understand and remember.

Chapter summary

- Pupils' engagement is crucial for science learning, though not a direct proxy for learning itself.
- Science capital encompasses an individual's science-related knowledge, attitudes, experiences and social contacts. It can influence engagement and aspirations in science.
- Strategies to improve science capital include good teaching practices, fostering science identity, and exposing students to diverse scientists and real-world applications.
- As curriculum leaders, it is our responsibility to ensure that our curriculums portray a diverse range of scientists.
- Citizen science projects offer practical engagement with real scientific research, enhancing relevance and skills.
- Storytelling in science education makes abstract concepts more accessible and memorable, leveraging the brain's affinity for narratives.

Questions for reflection

- Think about pupils' current attitudes towards science. How could we use the concept of science capital to help more pupils see science as 'for them' and potentially to aspire to scientific careers?
- Do we notice any patterns in terms of who participates in science lessons? Are there differences between boys' and girls' participation levels? Are there differences in the participation levels between pupils of different ethnicities?
- Reflecting on our current teaching practices, how can we better link everyday experiences to scientific concepts, to make science more relevant and engaging for our pupils?

- Reflect on the diversity of scientists represented in our current curriculum. How can I expand our current curriculum guidance to include a wider range of scientists from different backgrounds, genders and ethnicities?
- Which of the citizen science projects mentioned in the chapter interest me most? How might I integrate one of these projects into our curriculum to foster real-world scientific engagement?

Example PD session: exploring science careers

Here is an example of what a PD session on how to include discussion of science careers in lessons could look like.

TIMING SUGGESTION	SESSION GUIDANCE
Before the session	• Prepare copies of the article from Northumbria University on tackling stereotypical views of science careers (cited in the 'Explore further' section below). • Ask teachers to bring their plans for upcoming units' lessons.
10 mins	Ask teachers to read the article, and to share reflections on it.
5 mins	Use the 'Storytelling' section of this chapter to explain how storytelling can be effective pedagogy.
15 minutes	Ask teachers to look at their plans and identify where the lessons could highlight a specific career and/or include a story. (For example, a lesson on rocks could include a discussion on the career of palaeontology and the story of Mary Anning.)
15 minutes	• Ask teachers to draft their expositions introducing the career and/or telling the story. • Ask them to practise in pairs, giving one another feedback.

Explore further

- Ambition Institute's *Achieve and thrive: A research-based guide to pupil motivation and engagement* (2024) by S. Farndon: https://www.ambition.org.uk/pupil-engagement-guide/
- Books for Topics resources: https://www.booksfortopics.com/
- Storybook Science's *How to Use Stories to Teach Children About Science* (2022) by Clare Fearon
- King's College London's *Science Capital – an introduction* (video): https://www.youtube.com/watch?v=A0t70bwPD6Y
- Northumbria University's *Stereotypical views of scientists can be tackled in the classroom* (2021): https://www.northumbria.ac.uk/about-us/news-events/news/stereotypical-views-of-scientists-can-be-tackled-in-the-classroom/
- *Science Through Stories: Teaching Primary Science with Storytelling* (2022) by Jules Potter and Chris Smith
- STEM Learning's 'Inspiring scientists' resources: https://www.stem.org.uk/resources/collection/4372/inspiring-scientists?page=1
- STEM Learning's *Science capital made clear*: https://www.stem.org.uk/sites/default/files/pages/downloads/Science-Capital-Made-Clear.pdf
- Storytelling Schools resources: https://storytellingschools.com/
- University College London's *Primary Science Capital Project* resources (2021) by Nag Chowdhuri et al.: https://www.ucl.ac.uk/ioe/departments-and-centres/education-practice-and-society/research/stem-participation-social-justice-research/primary-science-capital-project

13 Implementing change

Implementation, in essence, is the process of putting a decision or plan into effect. For primary school science leaders, this concept is crucial as we continuously strive to improve our educational practices and outcomes for our science pupils. Schools are dynamic learning organisations that are constantly evolving. This evolution involves trying new approaches, learning from experiences and adopting the practices that prove most effective.

As science subject lead, you will likely need to implement changes to curriculum development, to improve science outcomes for pupils and to provide professional development for staff. It is also likely that you will be asked to write an action plan each year, outlining key priorities, actions and outcomes.

It is crucial to realise that the path to positive change is not always straightforward. In our eagerness to improve, we often introduce new ideas without fully considering how these changes will be managed, or what steps are necessary to maximise their chances of success. The 'who', 'why', 'where', 'when' and 'how' of implementation are frequently overlooked. This oversight can lead to well-intentioned projects fading away or being unsuccessful, as schools struggle to balance competing priorities.

Implementation doesn't always follow a neat, linear process. It can be full of surprises, setbacks and changes in direction. At times, it may feel more like a skilful art than a systematic process. Recognising these dynamics can help you to manage frustrations and view setbacks as natural features of the improvement journey.

Nevertheless, considering implementation as a system of small steps can be supportive. This chapter is intended to serve as a guide on how to do this, following the EEF guidance on stages of implementation. We'll go through each of the suggested stages step by step, providing a case study for each stage.

EEF stages of implementation

The EEF's guidance on implementation emphasises that successful implementation unfolds in stages over an extended period. It's not a single event that occurs when a decision is made or when training begins. Rather, it's a process that starts before the adoption decision and continues long afterwards.

The guidance segments this process into four key stages of successful implementation, each incorporating a series of steps. They are laid out in summary below.

EXPLORE
Step 1: Identify a priority.
Step 2: Make evidence-informed decisions about a solution to implement.
Step 3: Examine the solution's fit and feasibility regarding your context.
PREPARE
Step 4: Develop a clear, logical and well-specified implementation plan.
Step 5: Assess your school's readiness to deliver the implementation plan.
DELIVER
Step 6: Adopt a flexible and motivating leadership approach.
Step 7: Provide comprehensive follow-on support.
Step 8: Use implementation data actively, to tailor and improve the approach.
SUSTAIN
Step 9: Regularly review progress, and decide how to proceed.
Step 10: Maintain ongoing support and monitoring.

Careful consideration and planning in these areas are crucial because they allow for:

- clear goal-setting and alignment with school objectives
- efficient use of existing resources and structures
- better preparation for potential challenges
- increased buy-in from staff and stakeholders

- higher likelihood of sustainable, long-term change.

We are going to explore each of these stages and steps in more detail, alongside a case study of a science subject lead called Rhonda. Let's see how she goes through the steps of implementation to enact change in her school.

Explore

The first step of effective implementation is to explore an appropriate area for improvement, using a robust diagnostic process. Throughout this phase, it's crucial to involve key stakeholders to build shared ownership and leadership of the implementation process.

The phase involves several crucial steps.

Step 1: Identify a priority.

Identifying a priority requires gathering relevant and rigorous data from multiple sources, and generating plausible interpretations of that data. It's essential to challenge initial hunches and possible biases, and to examine the underlying issues behind surface-level problems.

For example, low attainment in Key Stage 2 science tests could be the outcome of an underlying issue such as poor-quality teaching and learning in science. This summary of data sources and their strengths and weaknesses adapted from Sharples et al. (2019, p.15) is useful to consider:

TYPE OF DATA	PROS	CONS	EXAMPLE OF GOOD USE
National test data	• Results are generally reliable as an overview. • Data are comparative. • Use involves no increased workload.	Overall scores can mislead interpretations of specific problems. (Question-level analysis can help.)	Use overall scores across year groups and over several academic years to provide reliable trend data.

TYPE OF DATA	PROS	CONS	EXAMPLE OF GOOD USE
Internal test data	• Tests can be tailored to specific needs. • Existing tests can be used. • Use is cheap and efficient.	• Data are often not as reliable as external tests. • Internal tests data cannot be compared to national norms.	Use to provide fine-grained insights on an issue alongside standardised test data.
Lesson observations	• Data give a holistic view of teachers' actions and pupils' learning responses.	• Results are potentially unreliable. • Presence of an observer can bias practice.	Use to observe the perceived issue in context and gain a richer picture of how pupils and teachers experience the issue.
Ofsted data	• Results allow comparisons with a national standard. • Ofsted gives an external perspective. • The report proposes actionable conclusions.	• Results are potentially unreliable. • High stakes can drive unhelpful actions. • Presence of an observer can bias practice.	Consider perceived issues raised on inspection in relation to your own school-improvement priorities.
Surveys and interviews	• Perceptions are considered. • Practice opens lines of communication. • Practice can be tailored to specific needs.	• Low response rates and pressure to respond mean data can be unreliable. • Use involves additional workload.	Use to understand the perceptions of a problem in context, and to gather suggestions for future actions.

Step 2: Make evidence-informed decisions about a solution to implement.

You can make evidence-informed decisions by drawing on both internal school insights and external evidence of what has worked in similar contexts. It's important to:

- build a rich evidence picture
- focus on how interventions are implemented as well as what they involve
- integrate research evidence with professional judgment.

Step 3: Examine the solution's fit and feasibility regarding your context.

It's important to examine whether the proposed change aligns with your school's needs and values. You should consider staff's motivation and skills, and evaluate the necessary structural changes.

The 'Explore' phase concludes with a decision to adopt a new programme or practice, setting the stage for the subsequent 'Prepare' phase.

Case study: running an 'Explore' phase

STEP	ACTIONS
1: Identify a priority.	• Rhonda is the science subject lead at a one-form-entry primary school in East London. She and her headteacher share a concern about how the progress of Pupil Premium (PP) pupils in science. They are not performing as well as their peers and, in the end-of-year science standardised tests, are performing below national standards. • Rhonda wants to find out more about the problem, so she conducts question-level analysis (QLA). She finds that a large proportion of PP pupils are struggling with vocabulary questions in particular. • She conducts a series of learning walks and lesson drop-ins, and does see explicit vocabulary instruction in each science lesson. However, there is no assessment for learning (AfL) performed afterwards: teachers are teaching vocabulary and then continuing the lesson without checking whether all pupils had understood. • Rhonda conducts a book-look and notices that key scientific terminology is often lacking in the answers of PP pupils.

STEP	ACTIONS
2: Make evidence-informed decisions about a solution to implement.	• Rhonda decides to start by refreshing her knowledge, using guidance from the EEF. The primary science report recommends both vocabulary instructions and AfL as important parts of science teaching. • Rhonda also reads the EEF's study on 'embedding formative assessment'. It looked at a large sample of 25,000 pupils and was given a high evidence-strength rating, but it was conducted in secondary schools. Rhonda knows she needs to be cautious applying data from secondary schools to primary schools. However, she also knows that AfL is a widely researched topic with a large evidence base.
3: Examine the solution's fit and feasibility regarding your context.	• Rhonda considers how embedding AfL specifically for vocabulary instruction would fit into the school's current science curriculum. • She concludes that teachers including AfL sessions after teaching vocabulary would be a feasible change to the current lesson structure. • She identifies teachers who are already using AfL successfully in other parts of their lessons, or in other subjects and those who might need extra support.

Prepare

The 'Prepare' phase is crucial in laying the groundwork for successful implementation. Throughout this phase, it's important to communicate clearly with all stakeholders, align the intervention with the school's mission and goals, and ensure that necessary resources and support systems are in place. By thoroughly preparing, schools can significantly increase the likelihood of successful implementation and, ultimately, improved outcomes.

Step 4: Develop a clear, logical and well-specified implementation plan.

There is no set way of laying out an implementation plan, but you should consider the following points.

- Why are you making the change in the first place? Define the problem and explain why you are solving it over others.
- What are you going to do? Define the strategy and its active ingredients (see below). Lay out what training and resources will be needed for its success.
- How will you know if it works? Decide how you will evaluate the process and the outcomes.

Active ingredients

- Active ingredients are the essential principles, practices and content that make an intervention effective. They are the core components that must be implemented with fidelity to achieve the desired outcomes.
- The more-clearly identified and well specified the active ingredients are, the more likely the programme or practice is to be implemented successfully. This specificity helps educators understand exactly what needs to be done.
- Effective active ingredients should be observable (easily seen and measured), replicable (applicable across different contexts) and irreducible (broken down to their most basic components).
- While active ingredients should be implemented consistently, it's important to identify which aspects of the intervention are tight (must be adhered to strictly) and which are loose (can be adapted to local context). This balance allows for necessary fidelity while permitting some flexibility in implementation.

Preparing for evaluation

- Leaders should look to conduct two types of evaluation of their strategies. One should consider how well the strategy was delivered (a process evaluation). The other should consider how well it may have worked (an outcome evaluation).
    - **Process evaluation**: Key areas to assess include acceptability (satisfaction with the intervention), feasibility (ease of delivery) and fidelity (how typically and well the intervention is being implemented).
    - **Outcome evaluation**: Select appropriate assessments to measure impact, such as national exams or internal assessments. To strengthen claims about effectiveness, use comparators like baseline assessments, control groups and/or comparable cohorts.

Step 5: Assess your school's readiness to deliver the implementation plan.

Assessing your school's readiness involves evaluating three key elements:

- the school's motivation
- its general capacity
- its innovation-specific capacity.

Based on this assessment, you can identify areas of strength to leverage and areas of weakness to address. This might involve additional preparation steps, such as providing preliminary training, securing additional resources or building staff buy-in. The table below suggests considerations for each element.

ELEMENT	EXPLANATION	CONSIDERATIONS
Motivation	The school's collective willingness to adopt the new intervention	• How well does the intervention align with the school's values and goals? • Are staff members aware of the need for change, and supportive of it? • Have you identified key stakeholders and opinion leaders who can champion the intervention?
General capacity	The overall functioning and resources of the school	• Does the school have stable leadership and staffing? • Are there effective communication channels in place? • Is there a culture of continuous improvement and openness to change? • Are there sufficient financial and time resources available?
Innovation-specific capacity	The particular resources needed for the specific intervention	• Do staff members have the necessary skills and knowledge to implement the intervention? • Is appropriate training available? • Are the required physical resources (such as space, equipment and technology) available? • Are there staff members who can provide ongoing support and coaching?

Case study: running a 'Prepare' phase

STEP	ACTIONS
4: Develop a clear, logical and well-specified implementation plan.	Rhonda writes her implementation plan for discussion with her line manager: • She defines the problem and the rationale. • She lays out the active ingredients of AfL strategies. • She plans out several implementation strategies, including professional development sessions and coaching pairs. • She plans her process evaluation: she will conduct lesson drop-ins to see whether AfL strategies are implemented, and with what levels of fidelity. • She plans her outcome evaluation: she will monitor vocabulary use in lesson drop-ins and book-looks, and monitor pupils' responses to vocabulary questions in end-of-unit quizzes and standardised end-of-year tests. • She lays out a clear timeline for implementation.
5: Assess your school's readiness to deliver the implementation plan.	• Rhonda identifies teachers who are already using AfL successfully in other parts of their lessons or in other subjects, and those who might need extra support. • She uses this information to assign coaching pairs. • She speaks to her line manager about other professional development sessions taking place during the year, and they decide appropriate times to introduce the AfL training.

In practice: an implementation plan

There is not one agreed way to lay out an implementation plan. However, it is important to set a plan and work through it methodically to ensure it is successful.

A plan for implementation could look like the example below, which uses a version of the EEF template.

PROBLEM (Why are you creating an implementation plan?)		
Teachers	**Pupils**	**Attainment**
Teachers are not checking for understanding after vocabulary teaching.	Some pupils are struggling with key vocabulary questions, or not using correct terminology in their classwork.	• PP pupils are not performing as well as their peers in standardised tests. • QLAs reveal that many of these pupils score least well on vocabulary questions.
INTERVENTION DESCRIPTION (What will your plan include?)		
Active ingredient 1	**Active ingredient 2**	**Active ingredient 3**
The correct Tier 2 and Tier 3 words will be chosen for explicit vocabulary teaching and assessment. These are the words that are most important for understanding the science topic and lessons.	Directly after vocabulary instruction, teachers will use a quick, low-stakes AfL strategy (such as mini-whiteboard responses or multiple-choice questions) to check for understanding.	Vocabulary from previous lessons will be included in retrieval practice at the start of the next lesson.
IMPLEMENTATION ACTIVITIES (How will your plan be implemented?)		
Training & support	**Monitoring**	**Educational materials**
• Teachers will receive consistent, iterative training over the course of the academic year, including a minimum of three dedicated PD sessions. • Less-experienced teachers will be paired up with more-experienced teachers in coaching pairs.	• You will conduct periodic lesson drop-ins and book-looks. • You will regularly check in with coaches. • Monitoring will remain a running agenda item in line management.	• All staff will have access to the books *Teach Like a Champion* by Doug Lemov and *Embedded formative assessment* by Dylan Wiliam. • The PLAN vocabulary progression documents will be shared with all staff.

IMPLEMENTATION OUTCOMES (How well is your plan being implemented?)		
Short term	Medium term	Long term
• Staff members will demonstrate an understanding of AfL theory and principles. • The majority of staff members will be able to draw on a range of practical strategies to support AfL. • The majority of staff members will experience a growing confidence in preparing AfL questions.	All staff will confidently and regularly use AfL strategies after vocabulary teaching.	• Curriculum and other planning will remain responsive and adaptive. • There will be a consistent, embedded approach to formative assessment.
FINAL OUTCOMES (What will be the ultimate goals of your plan?)		
Short term	Medium term	Long term
Pupils will achieve higher scores in vocabulary quizzes.	PP pupils will demonstrate higher attainment levels in end-of-unit quizzes.	PP pupils will demonstrate higher attainment levels in standardised end-of-year tests.

Deliver

The 'Deliver' phase is when the new programme or practice is applied for the first time. This often presents challenges as staff adapt to new ways of working.

Step 6: Adopt a flexible and motivating leadership approach.

As a leader, you should manage expectations and encourage buy-in. You should also be prepared to address both technical challenges (such as staff turnover or scheduling issues) and adaptive challenges (such as resistance or concerns).

Step 7: Provide comprehensive follow-on support.

This step includes:

- reinforcing initial training with expert coaching or mentoring, to help staff apply conceptual understanding to practical classroom behaviours
- complementing expert coaching with structured peer-to-peer collaboration, a focus on improving pupil outcomes, and implementation of effective professional learning communities with clear objectives.

Step 8: Use implementation data actively, to tailor and improve the approach.

You should regularly collect and analyse data on implementation outcomes to identify barriers and strengths. You will then be able to use this information to refine the intervention. Make thoughtful adaptations, but only when the active ingredients are securely understood and implemented. While local adaptations can be beneficial, it's crucial to maintain fidelity to the core components of the intervention.

Throughout this phase, it's important to view implementation as a learning process, continuously improving and refining the approach based on real-world experience and data.

Case study: running a 'Deliver' phase

STEP	ACTIONS
6: Adopt a flexible and motivating leadership approach.	• Having agreed the professional development programme with her headteacher, Rhoda holds an initial session to familiarise her colleagues with her implementation plan. • Rhonda starts by communicating the rationale for the change clearly to all science teachers, emphasising the potential benefits for PP pupils. • She acknowledges that implementing new strategies may be challenging at first, and reassures teachers that this is normal. • Rhonda remains available and accessible, regularly checking in with teachers to offer support and encouragement. • She celebrates early successes when teachers successfully incorporate AfL strategies into their vocabulary instruction, and praises these teachers publicly.
7: Provide comprehensive follow-on support.	• Rhonda creates a resource bank of AfL strategies specifically tailored for science vocabulary, which teachers can easily access and use. • She checks in with coaches regularly, to see if their coachees need further support.
8: Use implementation data actively, to tailor and improve the approach.	• During her lesson drop-ins, Rhonda notices that some teachers are struggling to fit AfL activities into the time allocated for vocabulary instruction. • Based on this observation, she works with teachers to develop quicker, more-efficient AfL strategies that can be incorporated easily into lessons.

Sustain

The 'Sustain' phase focuses primarily on maintaining the implemented changes. It could also involve acting on data to expand the changes' reach, or withdrawing the strategy.

Throughout this phase, it's crucial to remain flexible and responsive to changing contexts. Remember that even successful strategies may need to be scaled back or replaced as your school's needs evolve, or if better solutions become available. The goal is to create a culture of continuous improvement where evidence-based decision-making becomes the norm.

Step 9: Regularly review progress, and decide how to proceed.

Regularly review implementation and impact data to determine whether to continue, adjust, pause or withdraw the intervention.

- Be prepared to withdraw the strategy if it is not successful. Time, money and energy can then be redirected to more-effective strategies.
- If the strategy is successful, consider whether it could be expanded it to other departments, year groups or schools. Treat this scaling-up as a new implementation process, requiring preparation and training of its own.

Step 10: Maintain ongoing support and monitoring.

Continue to model expected behaviours, collect relevant data and make necessary adjustments. Continuously acknowledge, support and reward good implementation practices to maintain motivation and fidelity.

Case study: running a 'Sustain' phase

STEP	ACTIONS
9: Regularly review progress, and decide how to proceed.	• After six months, Rhonda conducts a thorough review of both process data and outcome data. • She finds that, while most teachers are consistently using AfL strategies for vocabulary, the impact on PP pupils' performances is mixed. • She is not sure that all teachers are acting on AfL data and adapting their teaching, or providing extra support for pupils who have not yet grasped the key vocabulary. • She decides to continue with the strategy, but also to return to Step 1 and gather more data to decide the next steps.

STEP	ACTIONS
10: Maintain ongoing support and monitoring.	• Rhonda continues to conduct periodic lesson observations and book-looks to monitor implementation and impact. • She ensures that training in AfL for science vocabulary is included in the induction for any new science teachers joining the school. • Rhonda regularly reports on the progress of the intervention to the school leadership team, maintaining their support for the ongoing initiative.

Chapter summary

- Schools are dynamic learning organisations that are constantly evolving and, as science lead, it is your role to guide improvement in approaches to your subject.
- The EEF's *Guide to Implementation* can help us to plan using through the four preparation and planning phases it specifies:
    - Explore: After identifying a priority, you should consider possible solutions in the light of expert research, school data and your school's context.
    - Prepare: Your plan should be carefully sequenced, and consider the 'why', 'what' and 'how' of the change being promoted. Buy-in from teachers is vital.
    - Deliver: You should action new approaches to teaching through comprehensive but flexible PD training, follow-up support and responsive feedback.
    - Sustain: It is important to review progress and continue monitoring to inform improvements to the approach.

Questions for reflection

- How do I currently identify priorities for improvement in my school, and how could I use a more data-driven approach?
- How well do staff members understand the 'active ingredients' of science-specific teaching strategies? How can I ensure clarity when implementing new strategies?
- In my context, what might be the barriers to the success of, and motivation for, change?

Explore further

- The EEF's *A School's Guide to Implementation* (2024) by J. Sharples, J. Eaton and J. Boughelaf
- The EEF's 'Examples of implementation plans' from an earlier version of *Putting Evidence to Work: A School's Guide to Implementation*: https://d2tic4wvo1iusb.cloudfront.net/production/eef-guidance-reports/implementation/EEF-Example-of-Implementation-Plans.pdf
- The EEF's: 'Implementation theme – active ingredients' from *Putting Evidence to Work: A School's Guide to Implementation*
- Evidence for Learning's *Insights into de-implementation* resources: https://evidenceforlearning.org.au/support-for-implementation/school-planning-and-recovery/de-implementation
- The Institute for Effective Education's *Engaging with Evidence Guide* (2019) by J. Haslam and A. Shaw
- *Thinking critically about educational claims* resources from That's a Claim!: https://thatsaclaim.org/educational/
- The University of Washington Department of Global Health's *What is implementation science?*

Bibliography

Allen, R (2018), 'What if we cannot measure pupil progress?' *Rebecca Allen*, www.rebeccaallen.co.uk/2018/05/23/what-if-we-cannot-measure-pupil-progress/

Almond, N. (2019), 'Ramble #6: Achieving coherence in primary science (Why primary science needs to be less like the Simpsons and more like Game of Thrones)' https://nutsaboutteaching.wordpress.com/2019/01/04/ramble-6-achieving-coherence-in-primary-science-why-primary-science-needs-to-be-less-like-the-simpsons-and-more-like-game-of-thrones/

Arc Education (nd), 'Literacy Teaching Toolkit'. *Arc*, arc.educationapps.vic.gov.au/learning/sites/literacy.

Archer, L., Moote, J., MacLeod, E., Francis, B., & DeWitt, J. (2020). *ASPIRES 2: Young people's science and career aspirations, age 10-19*. London: UCL Institute of Education.

Archer, L., DeWitt, J., Godec, S., Henderson, M., Holmegaard, H., Liu, Q., MacLeod, E., Mendick, H., Moote, J. and Watson E. (2023), ASPIRES 3 *Main Report*. London: UCL.

Ashbee, R. (2021) *Curriculum: Theory, Culture and the Subject Specialisms*. Abingdon: Routledge.

Asmussen, K., Charlton, J. and Law, J. (2017), *Language as a child wellbeing indicator*. London: Early Intervention Foundation (EIF).

Baddeley, A.D., Hitch, G. (1974), 'Working memory'. *Psychology of Learning and Motivation*, 8, 47–89.

Barton, C. and Bennett, T (ed.) (2019), *The researchED Guide to Education Myths: An evidence-informed guide for teachers*. London: John Catt.

Beck, I. L., McKeown, M. G. and Kucan, L. (2013), *Bringing Words to Life: robust vocabulary instruction* (2nd edition). New York: The Guildford Press.

Bianchi, L., Whittaker, C. and Poole, A. (2021), *The 10 key issues with children's learning in primary science in England*. Manchester and London: The University of Manchester and The Ogden Trust.

Biber, D., and Gray, B. (2017), *Grammatical complexity in academic English: Linguistic changes in writing*. Cambridge: Cambridge University Press.

Black, P. and Wiliam, D. (1998), 'Assessment and classroom learning'. *Assessment in Education* 5, 7 – 74.

Black, P. and Harrison, C. (2003), *Science Inside the Black Box: Assessment for Learning in the Science Classroom*.

Books for Topics (nd), *Books for Topics*, https://www.booksfortopics.com/.

Bower, G. H., & Clark, M. C. (1969), 'Narrative stories as mediators for serial learning'. *Psychonomic Science*, 14, 181–182.

Boxer, A. (2019), 'What's the big idea?' https://achemicalorthodoxy.co.uk/2019/05/15/whats-the-big-idea/.

Caviglioli, O. (nd), 'What is cognitive load theory?' https://www.teachwire.net/news/what-is-cognitive-load-theory/.

Caviglioli, O. (2019), *Dual Coding with Teachers*. London: John Catt.

Centre for Education Statistics and Evaluation (CESE) (2018), *Cognitive load theory in practice: Examples for the classroom*. Sydney: Centre for Education Statistics and Evaluation.

Centre for Industry Education Collaboration (CIEC) (2018), *Enabling Accurate Teacher Assessment in Primary Science*. York: CIEC.

Christodoulou, D. (2015), 'Why is teacher assessment biased?' *Daisy Christodolou*, www.daisychristodoulou.com/2015/11/why-is-teacher-assessment-biased/.

Clark, J. M., & Paivio, A. (1991), 'Dual coding theory and education'. *Educational Psychology Review*, 3(3), 149–210.

Cohen, M.T. and Johnson, H.L. (2012), 'Improving the acquisition and retention of science material by fifth grade students through the use of imagery interventions'. *Instr Sci* 40, 925–955.

Counsell, C. (2018), 'Taking curriculum seriously'. *Impact* 4.

Cowan, N. (2010), 'The magical mystery four: how is working memory capacity limited, and why?' *Curr Dir Psychol Sci* 19, 51–57.

Cuthbert, R. (2024), 'Unlocking the language of science: strategies for teaching science vocabulary'. *EEF blog*, https://educationendowmentfoundation.org.uk/news/eef-blog-unlocking-the-language-of-science-strategies-for-teaching-scientific-vocabulary.

De Bruyckere, P., Kirschner, P. A. and Hulshof, C. D. (2015), *Urban Myths and Learning and Education*. Oxford: Elsevier Academic Press.

Department for Education (DfE) (2015), *National curriculum in England: science programmes of study*. https://www.gov.uk/government/publications/national-curriculum-in-england-science-programmes-of-study

Department for Education (DfE) (2020), *Trends in International Mathematics and Science Study 2019: national report for England*. https://assets.publishing.service.gov.uk/government/uploads/system/uploads/attachment_data/file/941351/TIMSS_2019_National_Report.pdf

Department for Education (DfE) (2023), *PISA 2022: National Report for England*. https://www.gov.uk/government/publications/pisa-2022-national-report-for-england

Department for Education (DfE) (2024), *Early years foundation stage (EYFS) statutory framework* https://www.gov.uk/government/publications/early-years-foundation-stage-framework--2

Didau, D. and Rose, N. (2016) *What Every Teacher Needs to Know about Psychology*. London: John Catt.

Education Endowment Foundation (EEF) (2021), *Metacognition and Self-Regulated Learning: Guidance Report*. London: Education Endowment Foundation.

Evidence for Learning, (nd), 'Insights into de-implementation'. *Evidence for Learning*, evidenceforlearning.org.au/support-for-implementation/school-planning-and-recovery/de-implementation.

Farndon, S. (2024), 'Achieve and thrive: A research-based guide to pupil motivation and engagement'. *Ambition Institute*, www.ambition.org.uk/pupil-engagement-guide/.

Fearon, C. (2022), 'How to Use Stories to Teach Children About Science'. *Storybook Science*, https://storybookscience.co.uk/how-to-use-stories-to-teach-children-about-science/.

Fletcher Wood, H. (2017), 'Starting a lesson with Initial Stimulus Material'. *Improving Teaching*, improvingteaching.co.uk/2017/01/15/starting-a-lesson-withinitial-stimulus-material/.

Fountain, C. (2023), 'How to design a subject curriculum in 7 easy steps'. *Oak National Academy*, www.thenational.academy/blog/how-to-design-a-subject-curriculum.

Gilbert, J.K. and Justi, R. (2016), *Modelling-Based Teaching in Science Education*. London: Springer.

Gill, T. (2018), 'Writing Revolution Activities in Primary Science'. *Teach Well*, www.teach-well.com/writing-revolution-activities-in-primary-science/.

Grant, M. and Fisher, D. (2010), *Reading and Writing in Science: Tools to Develop Disciplinary Literacy*. London: Corwin.

Green, J. (2021), *Powerful Ideas of Science and How to Teach Them*. Abingdon: Routledge.

Harlen, W. and Allende, J. E. (ed) (2006), *Report on The Working Group on International Collaboration in The Evaluation of Inquiry-Based Science Education (IBSE) Programs*. Santiago: Fundacion para Estudios Biomedicos Avanzados de la Facultad de Medicina.

Haslam, J. and Shaw, A. (2019), *Engaging with Evidence Guide*. York: Institute for Effective Education. https://abbeyschool.co/php/admin/uploads/24/2019-10-19-1571487144-862183-IEE-Engaging-with-Evidence.pdf.

Harlen, W. (ed.) (2010), *Principles and Big Ideas of Science Education*. London: Association for Science Education. www.ase.org.uk.

Harlen, W. (ed.) (2015), *Working with Big Ideas of Science Education*. London: Association for Science Education.

Hattie, J. A. C. (2009), *Visible learning: A synthesis of over 800 meta-analyses relating to achievement*. Abingdon: Routledge.

Haynes, F. (2020), 'Disciplinary Literacy'. https://researchschool.org.uk/durrington/news/disciplinary-literacy-1.

Hochman, J. and Wexler, N. (2024), *The Writing Revolution*. San Francisco, CA: Jossey-Bass.

Holman, J. and Yeomans, E. (2018), *Improving Secondary Science Guidance Report*. London: EEF.

Howard, J. L., Bureau, J., Guay, F., Chong, J. X. Y., & Ryan, R. M. (2021), 'Student motivation and associated outcomes: a meta-analysis from self-determination theory'. *Perspectives on Psychological Science: a journal of the Association for Psychological Science*, 16(6).

Howard, P., Ioannou, K., Bailey, R., Prior, J. and Jay, T. (2018), 'Applying the science of learning in the classroom'. *Impact* 2: 9–12.

InterAcademy Partnership (IAP) (2021), *The Case for Inquiry-based Science Education – IBSE*. Trieste: The InterAcademy Partnership.

Jennings, A. (2024), *Vocabulary Ninja* (2nd edition). London: Bloomsbury.

Jerrim, J., Oliver, M. and Sims, S. (2022), 'The relationship between inquiry-based teaching and students' achievement. New evidence from a longitudinal PISA study in England'. *Learning and Instruction*, 80, 101310.

Johnstone, A.H. (1991), 'Why is science difficult to learn? Things are seldom what they seem'. *Journal of Computer Assisted Learning* 7(2):75–83.

King's College London (KCL) (nd), 'Science Capital – an introduction'. *KCL*, www.youtube.com/watch?v=A0t70bwPD6Y.

Kirby, J. (2014), 'How to design multiple- choice questions'. *Joe Kirby*, www.joe-kirby.com/2014/04/12/mcqdesign/.

Kirschner, P., Sweller, J. and Clark, R. (2006), 'Why minimal guidance during instruction does not work: an analysis of the failure of constructivist, discovery, problem-based, experiential, and inquiry-based teaching'. *Educational Psychologist* 41:2, 75–86.

Kirschner, P.A. and Hendrick, C. (2020) *How learning happens: seminal works in educational psychology and what they mean in practice*. Abingdon: Routledge.

Lawrence Hall of Science (nd), 'The Argumentation Toolkit'. *Lawrence Hall of Science*, argumentationtoolkit.lawrencehallof science.org/.

Lemke, J. L. (2004), 'The literacies of science' in Saul, E. W. (ed.), *Crossing borders in literacy and science instruction*. Newark, DE: International Reading Association, pp. 33–47.

Lemov, D. (2015), *Teach like a champion 2.0*. San Francisco, CA: Jossey-Bass.

Loxley, P., Dawes, L., Nicholls, L. and Dore, B. (2018), *Teaching Primary Science*. London: Routledge.

Luxton, K. and Pritchard, B. (2023), *Improving Primary Science Guidance Report*. London: Education Endowment Foundation.

Magaji, A. (2021), 'Promoting student-led questions in the secondary science classroom'. Impact, 12.

Major, L. & Higgins, S. (2019), *What works?: Research and evidence for successful teaching*. London: Bloomsbury Education.

Markwick, A. (2018), 'Developing literacy using science: prefixes and suffixes'. *Primary Science (Association of Science Education, ASE)*, 155:18-19. www.ase.org.uk.

McCrory, P. (2021), 'In defence of the classroom science demonstration'. *Hook Training*, hooktraining.com/defence- of-science-demonstrations/

Moje, E. B. (2008), 'Foregrounding the disciplines in secondary literacy teaching and learning: A call for change'. *Journal of Adolescent and Adult Literacy*, 52(2), 96–107.

Moore, J. (2020), 'Developing talk in the primary science classroom'. *Primary Science*, 2020: 12-16.

Myatt, M. and Tomsett, J. (2022), *Primary Huh: curriculum conversations with subject leaders in primary schools*. London: John Catt.

Nag Chowdhuri, M., King, H. and Archer, L. (2021), *The Primary Science Capital Teaching Approach: teacher handbook*. London: University College London.

Northumbria University (2021), 'Stereotypical views of scientists can be tackled in the Classroom'. Northumbria University, www.northumbria.ac.uk/about-us/news-events/news/stereotypical-views-of-scientists-can-be-tackled-in-the-classroom/.

Nuffield Foundation (2012), *Developing policy, principles and practice in primary school science assessment*. London: Nuffield Foundation.

Nuffield Foundation (2013), *Nuffield Practical Work for Learning: Argumentation*. London: Nuffield Foundation.

Nunes, T., Bryant, P., Strand, S., Hillier, J., Barros, R., and Miller-Friedmann, J. (2017), *Review of SES and Science Learning in Formal Educational Settings*. London: Education Endowment Foundation.

Oak National Academy (nd), 'KS1 & KS2 science curriculum'. *Oak National Academy*, www.thenational.academy/teachers/curriculum/science-primary/units.

Ofsted (2011), *Successful science: an evaluation of science education in England 2007—2010*. https://assets.publishing.service.gov.uk/government/uploads/system/uploads/attachment_data/file/413802/Successful_science.pdf.

Ofsted (2013), *Science education in schools: maintaining curiosity: a survey into science education in schools*. https://www.gov.uk/government/publications/maintaining-curiosity-a-survey-into-science-education-in-schools.

Ofsted (2020), *Annual Report 2018/19: HMCI Commentary*. www.gov.uk/government/publications/ ofsted-annual-report-201819-education-childrens- services-and-skills/ofsted-annual-report-201819-hmci- commentary.

Ofsted (2021), *Research review series: science*. https://www.gov.uk/government/publications/research-review-series-science/research-review-series-science.

Ogden Trust (nd), 'Resources'. *Ogden Trust*, www.ogdentrust.com/resources.

Ogden Trust (nd), 'Working scientifically resources'. *Ogden Trust*, www.ogdentrust.com/resources/?curriculum=&age=&series=working-scientifically.

Osborne, J., Simon, S. and Erduran, S. (2004), 'Enhancing the quality of argumentation in school science'. *Journal of Research in Science Teaching*, 41(10): 994–1020.

Osborne, J. and Dillon, J. (eds) (2010), *Good Practice in Science Teaching: What research has to say*, Maidenhead: Open University Press.

Pashler, H., Bain, P., Bottge, B., Graesser, A., Koedinger, K., McDaniel, M. and Metcalfe, J. (2007), *Organizing Instruction and Study to Improve Student Learning*. Washington, DC: National Center for Education Research, Institute of Education Sciences.

Perry, T., Lee, R., Rübner, C., Cordingley, P., Shapiro, K. and Youdell, D. (2021), *Cognitive science approaches in the classroom: a review of the evidence*. London: EEF.

PLAN (2021), 'Knowledge Matrices'. *PLAN*, www.planassessment.com/knowledge-matrices-teacher.

PLAN (2021), 'Science subject leader'. *PLAN*, www.planassessment.com/science-subject-leader.

Potter, J. and Smith, C. (2022), Science Through Stories: *Teaching Primary Science with Storytelling*. Independently published.

Primary Science Teaching Trust (PSTT) (nd), 'Common Misconceptions'. *PSTT*, pstt.org.uk/resources/common-misconceptions/.

Primary Science Teaching Trust (PSTT) (nd), 'Types of Enquiry'. *PSTT*, pstt.org.uk/resources/enquiry-approaches/.

Qualter, A and Harlen, W. (2014), *The Teaching of Science in Primary Schools* (6th edition). London: Taylor & Francis.

Quigley, A. (2018), *Closing the Vocabulary Gap*. Abingdon: Routledge.

Quigley, A. and Coleman, R. (2021), *Improving Literacy in Secondary Schools*. London: EEF.

ResearchED (2020) 'Jon Hutchinson: Seven Distinctions Every Subject Leader Should Know About'. https://www.youtube.com/watch?v=RAhVhlaNQlc.

ResearchEDHome (2020), 'Adam Boxer: Dual Coding for Teachers Who Can't Draw: Teacher's Explanations'. *ResearchEdHome*, www.youtube.com/watch?v=16SBht2iF_k.

Roberts, J. (2022), 'Helping learners think like scientists – why Cambridge Primary and Lower Secondary Science now puts more emphasis on scientific modelling'. *Cambridge International*, blog.cambridgeinternational.org/scientificmodelling/.

Rosenshine, B. (2012), 'Principles of instruction: research-based strategies that all teachers should know'. *American Educator* 36 (1): 12–19.

Roy, P., Chiat, S., and Dodd, B. (2014), *Language and Socioeconomic Disadvantage: From Research to Practice*. London: City University London.

Scarborough, H. S. (2001), 'Connecting early language and literacy to later reading (dis)abilities: Evidence, theory and practice' in Neuman, S. & Dickinson, D. (eds.) *Handbook for researching early literacy* (pp. 97–110). New York, NY: Guildford Press.

Science Sparks (nd), 'Science Experiments for Kids'. *Science Sparks*, www.science-sparks.com.

Sealy, C. (ed) (2020), *The researchED guide to The Curriculum: An evidence-informed guide for teachers*. London: John Catt.

Shanahan, T., and Shanahan, C. (2008), 'Teaching disciplinary literacy to adolescents: Rethinking content-area literacy'. *Harvard Education Review*, 78(1), 40–59.

Shanahan, T., and Shanahan, C. (2012). 'What is disciplinary literacy and why does it matter?' *Topics in Language Disorders*, 32, 1–12.

Shanahan, T. (2019), 'Disciplinary Literacy in the Primary School'. Shanahan on Literacy, https://www.shanahanonliteracy.com/publications/disciplinary-literacy-in-the-primary-school.

Sharples, J., Albers, B, Fraser, S and Kime, S. (2019), *A School's Guide to Implementation* (2nd edition). London: Education Endowment Foundation.

Sharples, J., Eaton, J. Boughelaf, J. (2024), *A School's Guide to Implementation* (3rd edition). London: Education Endowment Foundation.

Sherrington, T. and Stafford, S. (2018), *An introduction to schemas and why your students can't have too much knowledge*. London: The Chartered College of Teaching.

Skinner, E., Furrer, C., Marchand, G., and Kindermann, T. (2008), 'Engagement and disaffection in the classroom: art of a larger motivational dynamic?' *Journal of Educational Psychology*, 100(4), 765–781.

Smith, K. (2016), *Working Scientifically: A Guide For Primary School Teachers*. Abingdon: Routledge.

Standards and Testing Agency (2019), 'Key stage 2 science sampling 2018: methodology note and outcomes' https://www.gov.uk/government/publications/key-stage-2-science-sampling-2018-methodology-note-and-outcomes.

STEM Learning (nd), 'Science capital made clear'. *STEM Learning*, www.stem.org.uk/sites/default/files/pages/downloads/Science-Capital-Made-Clear.pdf.

STEM Learning (nd.), 'Inspiring scientists'. *STEM Learning*, www.stem.org.uk/resources/collection/4372/inspiring-scientists.

STEM Learning (2009), *Getting Practical: a Framework for Practical Work in Science*. SCORE.

Stern, J. (2019), 'What is schema? How do we help students build it?' *Education Week* https://www.edweek.org/teaching-learning/opinion-what-is-schema-how-do-we-help-students-build-it/2019/10.

Storytelling Schools (nd), 'Storytelling Schools resources'. *Storytelling Schools*, storytellingschools.com/.

Strong, J. and Corbett, P. (2024), 'How Talk for Writing Supports Science'. *Talk for Writing*, https://www.talk4writing.com/wp-content/uploads/2024/03/TfW-Science.pdf.

Such, C. (2021), 'Curriculum Giveaway 2.0 – Science'. *Primary Colour*, www.primarycolour.home.blog/2021/04/07/curriculum-giveaway-2-0-science/.

Such, C. (2021), *The Art and Science of Teaching Primary Reading*. London: Sage.

Tao, P. K. (1994), 'Words that matter in science: A study of Hong Kong students comprehension of non-technical words in science'. *Educational Research Journal*, 9 (1): 1–23.

That's a Claim! (nd), 'Thinking critically about educational claims resources'. *That's a Claim!*, thatsaclaim.org/educational/.

The Royal Society (2014), *Vision for Science and Mathematics Education*. London: The Royal Society.

Tracy, C. (2018), 'Guidelines for future physics curricula'. *School Science Review*, 100 (370): 36–43.

Uchihara, T., Webb, S. and Yanagisawa, A. (2019), 'The Effects of Repetition on Incidental Vocabulary Learning: A Meta-Analysis of Correlational Studies'. *Language Learning*, 69 (3): 559 – 599.

University College London (UCL) (nd), 'Primary Science Capital Project'. *UCL*, www.ucl.ac.uk/ioe/departments-and-centres/educationpractice-and-society/research/stem-participation-social-justice-research/primary-science-capital-project

University of Colorado Boulder (nd), PhET Interactive Simulations. *PhET*, https://phet.colorado.edu/.

University of Washington Department of Global Health (nd), 'What is implementation science?'. *University of Washington Department of Global Health*, impsciuw.org/implementation-science/learn/implementation-science-overview.

Wellcome Trust (2017), *'State of the nation' report of UK primary science education*. Leicester: CFE Research.

Wexler J., Mitchell, M. A., Clancy, E. E. and Silverman, R. D. (2016), 'An investigation of literacy practises in high school science classrooms'. *Reading and Writing Quarterly* 33 (3): 258–277.

Wiggins, G. P. and McTighe, J. (2005), *Understanding by Design* (2nd edition). Alexandria, VA: Association of Supervision and Curriculum Development (ASCD).

Wiliam, D. (2013), *Principled Curriculum Design*. London: SSAT.

Wiliam, D. (2014), *Principled assessment design*. London: SSAT.

Wiliam, D. (2017), *Embedded Formative Assessment* (2nd edition). Bloomington, IN: Solution Tree Press.

Willingham, D. T. (2009), 'Why Don't Students Like School?' *American Educator* 33(1):4–13.

Willingham, D. T. (2021), *Why Don't Students Like School?* (2nd edition). San Francisco, CA: Jossey-Bass.

Young, M., Lambert, D., Roberts, C., and Roberts, M. (2014), *Knowledge and the Future School: Curriculum and Social Justice*. London: Bloomsbury.

Index

academic talk 121–2, 126
active ingredients, in change implementation 165, 168, 170
activity-based curriculum design 41
analogies 81
argumentation 123–5
assessment
  and curriculum objectives 63
  feedback effectiveness 64
  formative assessment strategies 67
  integration with teaching 63
  manageability 64
  methods 64, 66
  misconceptions see misconceptions
  preconceptions 69–70
  of prior knowledge 68–9
  purpose of 63
  reliability 64–5
  statutory guidance 65–6
  validity 64–5
Association for Science Education (ASE) 14, 107
attitudes 143

backward-planning
  reports writing 54–5
  for the topic of cells 53–4
  for the topic of plants 55–7
behaviour, during practical activities 109–10
big ideas
  definition of 23–4
  Harlen's big ideas 25–7
  keystone concept of 24, *25*
  powerful knowledge 27–8
  in primary science 34–6
  problems with 32–3
  schemas 28–32, *29*, *30*

change implementation
  active ingredients 165
  deliverance 169–71
  EEF stages of 160–1
  evaluation preparation 165
  evidence-informed decisions in 162–3
  exploration 161–4
  follow-on support 170
  implementation data usage 170–1
  leadership approach 169
  ongoing support and monitoring maintenance 172–3
  plan 164–5
  plan delivery 166–9
  preparation 164–9
  priority identification 161–2
  progress review and decision to proceed 172
  solution's fit and feasibility 163–4
  sustenance 171–3
Chartered College of Teaching, The 14
citizen research projects 151–2
claim 123–4
clear instructions writing 137
cognitive conflict 74
cognitive demands, management of 19
cognitive overload 18, 80
cognitive science 18–20
colleagues support 4, 70
concept cartoons 119–20
concrete resource, as stimulus 118
Consortium of Local Education Authorities for the Provision of Science Services (CLEAPSS) 107–8
construct validity 65
content knowledge 66
content validity 65
coverage-focused curriculum design 41
curriculum

aims of 42–3
areas covered 2
development 3
impact 40
implementation 40
intent 39
meaning of 39–40
objectives 63
curriculum design and planning 41–2
  aims of curriculum 51–2
  and disciplinary knowledge 43–4, 53–7
  importance of sequencing 44–7
  key features mapping 58–9
  knowledge organisers 61–2
  long-term plans 57–8
  medium-term plans 59–62
  mistakes in 41
  need for detail 47–8
  schemes of work 40
  starting with the end points 52–3
  and substantive knowledge 43, 44, 53–7

data, and arguments 123–4
deliverance, in change implementation 169–71
demonstrations 111–12, 119
diagnostic questions, in assessment 71–3
dialogue
  academic talk 121–2
  advantages of 115
  argumentation 123–5
  routines for 116–17
  stimuli for 118–21
Directed Activities Related to Text (DARTs) 132
disciplinary knowledge 43–4, 53–7
disciplinary literacy
  access to scientific texts 132–3
  composing explanations and information texts 134
  investigation reports 134–5
  key features 130–1
  results 136
  in science 130–1
  science-specific texts, reading of 131–3
  scientific language features 131
  scientific methods 136–8?
  writing scientifically 133–8
dual coding 79–80

educational challenges
  challenges at school 6–7
  international comparisons 6
  national attainment data 6
  school leadership challenges 7
Education Endowment Foundation (EEF) 13, 17
  enquiry skills, seven-step model for 108–9
  stages of implementation 160–1
Education Reform Act of 1988 2
engagement, in science
  citizen research projects 151–2
  diverse range of scientists 144–50
  science capital 141–4
  storytelling 152–5
'Engaging with evidence guide' (Institute for Effective Education) 13
enquiry skills
  and enquiry-based learning 103
  terminology 102
  types of 103–6
evaluation, in change implementation 165
evidence-based judgement 66
evidence-informed decisions, in change implementation 162–3
existing knowledge 19, 28, 68
experiences 143
expert schema 30
explanations and information texts, in scientific writing 134
exploration, in change implementation 161–4
Explorify 16

face validity 65
fluency, development of 19
focus, finding 5

follow-on support, in change implementation 170
formative assessment 67, 115
frequent recall 19

gender disparities 8

Harlen's big ideas 25–7
historical models 81

inequities in science education 7–8
Institute for Education Sciences (IES) 14
Institute of Physics (IOP) 15
international comparisons, of science scores 6
investigation reports, in scientific writing 134–5

knowledge organisers 61–2

language of science
    limited focus on authors 131
    multi-modal expression 131
    noun-heavy 130
    passive voice 130
leadership approach, in change implementation 169
learning, in research evidence 18
long-term memory 18
macroscopic knowledge 82

misconceptions 70–1
    challenging 73–5
    and diagnostic questions 71–3
modelling
    dual coding 79–80
    limitations and evaluation of 83–5
    macroscopic knowledge 82–3
    model types 80–2, 81
    submicroscopic knowledge 82
    symbolic knowledge 82
    usage of 82
moderation, in assessment 66
monitoring, in change implementation 172–3

national attainment data 6
National Curriculum for England 2
novice schema 29

'Odd one out' activities 120
Ogden Trust 15
ongoing support, in assessment 66
optimising load 18, 21

physical models 81
PLAN: Planning for Assessment 16
planning, in research evidence 19
plausible distractors 71
poems, as stimulus 118
practical science
    behaviour, during practical activities 109–10
    demonstrations 111–12
    enquiry skills 102–6
    importance of 101–2
    principles of 106–10
    safety guidance 107–9
preparation, in change implementation 164–9
primary education sources and guidance 13–14
primary science leader 2–3
    colleagues support 4
    curriculum development 3
    resourcing 3
    science and enrichment 4–5
    teaching and learning 4
Primary Science Teaching Trust (PSTT) 15
prioritisation 5
priority identification, in change implementation 161–2
prior knowledge assessment
    reasons for 68
    strategies for 68–9
progress review, in change implementation 172

racial disparities 8
research evidence
    Chartered College of Teaching 14

cognitive science 18–20
contexts comparison 12
Education Endowment Foundation (EEF) 13
educational fallacies 12–13
Institute for Education Sciences (IES) 14
large-scale studies 11
participants consistency 11–12
primary education sources and guidance 13–14
results 12
science-specific resources 14–17
simplification 12
resourcing 3
results, in scientific writing 136
routines, in dialogue and support oracy 116–17
Royal Institute 16
Royal Society of Biology (RSB) 15
Royal Society of Chemistry (RSC) 15

safety guidance, in practical science activities 107–9
scale models 81
schemas 28–32
school leadership challenges 7
school leadership challenges 7
science and enrichment 4–5
science capital 141–4
science education, importance of 2
science-specific resources 14–17
science-specific texts, reading of 131–3
scientific knowledge, levels of 82–3
scientific knowledge levels 82–3
scientific methods, in scientific writing 136–8
scientific texts, access to 132–3
scientists, diverse range of 144–50
sequencing, in curriculum planning 44–7
simulations 81
social contacts 143

socio-economic disadvantage 7–8
spaced retrieval 19
statutory guidance, in assessment 65–6
STEM Learning 15
stimuli, for discussion 118–21
stories, as stimulus 118
stories sourcing
    creating stories 154–5
    finding science stories 154
    links with well-known stories 153–4
storytelling 152–5
submicroscopic knowledge 82
substantive knowledge 43, 44, 53–7
support, in change implementation 172–3
support levels, in research evidence 19
sustenance, in change implementation 171–3
symbolic knowledge 82

teacher assessment 66
Teacher Assessment Frameworks 65
teaching strategies
    consolidation 97
    explanation 94–6
    exploration 96–7
timetable challenges 6–7

visual models 81
vocabulary
    important of 89–90
    teaching strategies 94–7
    tier of words 90–3

warrants 123–4
'What if …' questions 120
Willingham's 4Cs guideline for stories 154–5
working memory 18
work schemes, in curriculum planning 40
writing scientifically 133–8